BEFORE THE WEDDING BELLS

Preparing for a Lasting & Fulfilling Marriage

Sam and Mary George

Authentic

HYDERABAD · COLORADO SPRINGS

Before the Wedding Bells
by Sam & Mary George

Copyright © 2010 by Sam & Mary George

First edition 2010
ISBN: 978-81-7362-998-3

Published by
Authentic Books

P. O. Box 2190, Secunderabad 500 003, Andhra Pradesh.
www.authenticindia.in

1820 Jet Stream Drive, Colorado Springs, CO 80921, USA.
www.authenticbooks.com

Unless otherwise noted, Scripture quotations are taken from the Holy Bible, *New International Version*®. NIV®. Copyright © 1973, 1978, 1984 by the International Bible Society. Used by permission of Zondervan Publishing House. All rights reserved.

Authentic Books is an imprint of Authentic Media, the publishing division of Biblica South Asia.

Printed and bound in India by
Authentic Media, Secunderabad 500 055

Commendable Acclaims. . .

Marriage is a divine sacrament and essentially human. Today, many young people are afraid to enter into married life for the very reason that lots of marriages are ending in divorce. In such a scenario in the church and society, I am happy to recommend the marriage preparation book *Before the Wedding Bells* for use by pastors, counselors and small group leaders. I appreciate Sam & Mary George for publishing this book for wider use, in twelve practical lessons with several examples of real life stories. May this be blessing to all.

The Rt. Rev. Dr. Geevarghese Mar Theodosius
Bishop, The Mar Thoma Church.

A timely resource for a new generation entering into marriage. Every pastor and parent must ensure that all engaged couples go through this curriculum before they get married.

The Rt. Rev. Dr. George Ninan
Chair, Christian Institute for
South Asian American Concerns (USA)

In a world where marriages and families are finding it difficult to cope with new challenges I congratulate the authors and publishers for this helpful and timely handbook. I urgently recommend the use of *Before the Wedding Bells* and pray it receives wide-ranging and welcome audiences.

The Rt. Rev. Vijay Sathe
Bishop, Pune Diocese, Church of North India

An excellent tool, with a judicious combination of principles and practical tips, for those who want to enter into marriage and family life and to make the most of this wonderful gift from the source of all goodness and blessings, God himself. *Before the Wedding Bells* is also an outflow of the beauty and richness of a couple's family life; it is an act of noble sharing with a passionate commitment to the truth and the young people of this generation. A must read for all those who seriously consider marriage and family because every chapter in this book "matters."

Most Rev. Dr. C. V. Mathew
Presiding Bishop, St. Thomas Evangelical Church of India

Sam George has addressed a heart-felt need in the Asian community, where pre-marital counseling was non-existent until recently. Even now, culturally compatible resource materials are hard to find. Sam and Mary's commitment to protect the "parivar" (family) is reflected throughout the book.

Rev. Dr. Sunny Philip
Chairman, Global Network of Christian Indian Leaders (USA)

There is a huge difference between a wedding and a marriage. The wedding is that initial expensive event and investment—marriage gets even more expensive for the rest of your life. Marriage consists of the more extravagant intangible expenses of life. Marriage will cost you who you are because one must be willing to deny one's self in deference and honor of the other. That is why *Before the Wedding Bells* is so important.

Dr. Samuel R. Chand (USA)
www.samchand.com

In India preparation for the wedding day is of greater importance than preparing for marriage itself. In the current context when the institution of marriage is attacked from every side, it's very crucial for every young adult to prepare for marriage. This book serves couples who are serious about building their marriage on the solid foundation of God's Word.

P.C. Mathew and Ciby Mathew
National Directors
Urban India Ministries, Bangalore (India)
www.UrbanIndia.org

Sam and Mary have done an excellent job in bringing out this valuable book for couples who are planning to get married. This will be a helpful tool for them that would strengthen their family life, the church and the society. Sam and Mary are assets for the kingdom of God because their contribution is precious, timely and practical.

Rev. Dr. J.N. Manokaran
Managing Director
Trainers of Pastors International Coalition (India)

Sam and Mary's book unveils that marriage is divine in origin, divine in pattern and divine in purpose. It renders a blueprint from the heart of God to build a godly Christian home. An excellent read!

Dr. Joseph Paturi
President, Temple Baptist College
Cincinnati (USA)

This book *Before the Wedding Bells* contains a rich reservoir of theoretical principles and practical advice towards building a rock-solid fulfilling marriage—a life together that will be the best it can be. The warm personal quality of Sam and Mary George's writing has the impact of intimate conversations with a wise friend and counselor. I highly recommend this marriage handbook as a gift for couples embarking on their adventure of marriage and family life.

Pastor Pritam Singh Sandhu
Founder, South Asian Connection (Singapore)
www.southasianconnection.com

The dating of two individuals over a period of time in the Western world and meeting of prospective groom and bride before the wedding in the Eastern world are meant to explore the mutual chemistry and compatibility. Unfortunately many do not zero in on the critical issues which often result in divorces in the West and/or living as strangers under the same roof in the East. Sam and Mary who know the West and the East have written *Before the Wedding Bells* to save marriages of all prospective couples. Having journeyed together for 32 years, we highly commend this book.

Pramila and K. Rajendran
India Missions Association (India)

We are thrilled to see this excellent resource written specifically for the Asian family culture. Having worked with Indian families both in North and South India for the last 30 years, and now with Chinese, we believe *Before the Wedding Bells* fills a huge need as the Asian family culture is becoming more and more international.

Rod and Ruthie Gilbert
Authors of *Marriage Masala* (Hong Kong)

The secret of "happy ever after" is not merely to start with extravagant celebrations but, more importantly, to continue making the best possible investments in what can and should be a lifetime of intimate relationship. Here is a book packed with profound insights and practical tips. An excellent gift for anyone considering marriage, or actually in it!

Prabhu Guptara
Distinguished Professor of Global Business
William Carey University, Meghalaya (India)
www.prabhu.guptara.net

Numerous volumes on Christian marriage and family have appeared but mostly from a Western perspective. Sam and Mary George have met a critical need with both Western and Asian perspectives. What is strikingly unique about their book is the biblical and practical ways they discuss and challenge contemporary cultural alternatives, while providing the Designer's directives. This volume is not just full of new information; it is also a powerful tool for marriage and family transformation.

Rev. Dr. Martin Alphonse
Associate Professor, Multnomah University, Portland (USA)

One of the greatest evidence that we have been transformed by the power of the Gospel is that our marriages and families reflect the character of God. When they reflect a true community of love, respect and open communication, people around us will witness what Jesus taught about loving one another. Sam and Mary write from years of experience and ministry amongst couples and I am sure this book will help readers to get closer to God, spouse and family, and be a light that shines in their places of work and neighborhood.

Rev. Dr. Timothy P. Svoboda
Youth with a Mission, San Francisco (USA)

When it comes to marriage, it does "pay to prepare"! This premarital text takes faith and cultural values seriously to build a Christian home. This is a key resource for pastors, caregivers and counselors. But a must read for those planning to be married.

Chris Gnanakan, DMin, PhD
Director of Training, Outreach To Asia Nationals (USA)

Contents

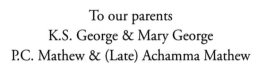

To our parents
K.S. George & Mary George
P.C. Mathew & (Late) Achamma Mathew

Acknowledgment

We are grateful to many people for their contributions to this book. We want to thank our mentor Dr. T.V. Thomas for his guidance and encouragement throughout this project. We are indebted to all endorsers for their kind and encouraging words.

We thank the board and staff of Parivar International in releasing me to pursue this writing project amidst a busy season of ministry. We are grateful to Matthew & Anita Philip, P.C. & Ciby Mathew, Dr. Mabel Koshy, Shoji Boldt, Dr. Thomas Kulanjiyil and Dr. Jacob & Darly Philip for reading drafts of the manuscripts and giving me insightful inputs and criticisms. We are deeply grateful to Shiji Mathew and Priya Varghese for their thoughtful editorial comments. Special thanks to Abraham "Joe" Thomas for field testing this material in premarital camps.

We are also thankful to many engaged couples who went through this curriculum in its early form and their feedbacks shaped much of this book. We owe a great deal to couples who have shared their hearts to us and have taught us much about marriage. We want to express our thanks to our mentors for the many relationship skills and insights they have taught us. Much of this evolved out of a deep conviction that good relationship takes work and it can begin even before you are married.

Writing a book as a couple is never easy. Finding time and guilt of neglecting children are a real challenge. We are grateful to our parents and friends who stepped in to carry out household chores and took care of our two wonderful boys. This writing project also forced us to reflect on our own marriage preparation efforts. We had lots of conversation about early days of our relationship, read through journal entries and interviewed engaged and newly married couples, each of which was an extremely enriching experience.

Most importantly we thank God for bringing us together in marriage and teaching these lessons first hand. Marriage is an amazing adventure worth every effort and preparation.

Preface

With nearly half of all new marriages in the West ending in divorce, more couples are careful before entering into it. They want to make sure it is the right decision, and they want to do everything they can within their capacity hoping to increase their chances of marital success. *Before the Wedding Bells* is a resource intended for singles who are pursuing a relationship or for engaged couples counting down to the big day in their lives. This is designed to assist individuals and couples to develop a deeper understanding of marriage and to develop relational skills to navigate their way through marriage successfully.

As the adage goes, 'failing to prepare is preparing to fail.' It is true of marriage as for anything else. One marriage enrichment expert once remarked, "Marriage is the deepest and potentially the most gratifying of all human relationships, but it is also one of the most demanding. Unfortunately couples seldom have more preparation than a little advice from their parents and a new set of china." Many young couples' expectations of marriage revolve around the false belief that love will get them through rough times.

While love is important, it won't be enough if couples don't have the basic attitudes and skills they need for a successful marriage. Lasting marriages require partners who respect one another, who have gained knowledge about what makes marriage work, and who have developed skills that will enhance the relationship.

We sincerely believe in the benefit of marriage preparation. Months before we got married, we ran into some excellent marriage preparation resources, which had a significant impact on our marriage, and we continue to reap its benefits after fourteen years. Ever since, we have been helping people, both singles and married couples, to understand marriage.

This book also came out of marriage preparation workshops that we have conducted in many cities of India and United States. Unlike many other resources for marriage preparation, this takes a unique cultural and philosophical perspective of Asian Indians and also has been used among other ethnic and linguistic groups. It is based on a Christian worldview, but is applicable for people of all faiths. It is practical, time-tested, insightful and most of all very useful.

Our purpose of writing this book can be summarized as:

- To understand what marriage really is and to gain a realistic view of marriage
- To help you understand yourself, your mate and your future together
- To develop some basic relationship skills
- To avoid many of the pitfalls that couples tend to fall into
- To help you get a great start to your married life

This is meant for young adults who are seriously considering marriage, engaged couples and all those who work with them like relationship mentors, counselors, premarital counselors, priests, pastors and small group leaders. It can be used for individual perusal, but best used along with your mate (if you are in a committed relationship). The first two chapters are more geared towards singles and those exploring serious relationship. However, engaged couples could read through first two chapters to review foundational realationship principles. The engaged couple may skip over to chapter three, but there is no harm to reading through first two chapters. The book could also be used as a small group resource and premarital training curriculum. As you work through pages of this book, we suggest you do so with a pastor, a counselor, a mature couple or a small group.

All names in the stories are changed to protect the identities, and some of them are fictional in order to bring out certain truths. There are several examples of real life scenarios couples face. We hope and pray you will find it useful and will build a lasting and very fulfilling marriage.

1

Love Matters
Finding the Love of Your Life

Love is blind; Marriage is an eye-opener. (Unknown)

Live happily with the woman you love through the fleeting days of your life. (Ecclesiastes 9:9 TLB)

"I am in love!" announced Anita over the phone excitedly. Anita is a college-going young lady in our neighborhood and is actively involved in a nearby church youth group.

"That's great!" I replied, "Tell me more about this wonderful person. Where did you meet him? How do you know he is the man for you? Why do you want to spend the rest of your life with him? What have you both decided about your future?"

After a brief silence thinking over my questions, she responded, "I don't know. It feels so right when I talk to him. It is great to be around him. I simply know he is the guy for me. I am in love, you see!"

Love is one of the most used and abused words in English language. Poetries, steamy romance novels, movies, advertisements and now internet are rife with its usage. People use the word in a variety of different contexts—what they like (I love coffee) or how they feel (I love my pet dog) or romantic feeling towards someone special (I am attracted to someone) and even talking about sex (making love). Many confuse love with a childhood crush, tingling sensation or attraction to a collegemate. Some mistake infatuation with love, while others jump into bed seeking love. On the other hand one can find many loveless marriages and others who seek love relationships outside of marriage.

In "arranged marriages" you marry first and then fall in love with your spouse afterward. In "love marriages" you fall in love first and then marry. Whether love follows or precedes the wedding, it is an integral part of every relationship. Whatever be the case, love is an essential to building strong fulfilling marital bond. Let us take a quick look at what love is not, before understanding what love truly is.

What Love Is Not

Love is not merely a *feeling*. Young people often get caught up in an intense exhilarating emotion and call it love. They mistake the warm fuzzy sensation when they run into someone at school, mall, church or temple etc to be love. Feelings are important in the marital relationship, but emotions alone cannot be the basis of fulfilling marriage. A young lady wrote this love poem:

He held me close
A chill ran down my spine
I thought it was love
But it was just his ice cream melting!

Love is not *infatuation*. During adolescence and young adulthood attraction to someone of the opposite sex is quite natural. In fact, if you do not feel attracted to someone of opposite sex, you have a much more serious problem! Some parents and cultural biases try to contain such attraction to be socially inappropriate, which can be harmful in gender identity development. See the table on the next page about how infatuation differs from love. The table is compiled from various relationship resources.

Many singles believe that love is a tingling **sensation** based on physical and emotional attraction. Some have called it puppy love—a kind of overwhelming sense of attraction based primarily on visual allure, generated when a potential mate appears on their radar. This happens when your "prince charming comes riding on a white horse" sweeping you off your feet or when you madly fall in love with a "princess" of your dreams. True love is much more than that.

Some mistake love to be endless **romance**. After marriage, a couple may wonder whatever happened to romance and the notion of how they need to feel about intimate relationships. Bollywood films have tainted our view of marriage, and we expect our spouse will run around trees and sing love songs to us! Just as easily one can feel this way, it can quickly and easily vanish also. The enchanting sense can quickly degenerate when the magic just isn't there

We come to love not by finding a perfect person, but by learning to see an imperfect person perfectly.
– Unknown

anymore. If you fall in love, you can also fall out of it. When swept off your feet, it is hard to find your footing again. Ancient Greeks compared falling in love to going insane!

Love is not **sex**. In today's promiscuous culture, people are exchanging body fluids before exchanging their names. People want to get into the act, desire intimate experiences and think everybody is doing it anyway—all in the name of "love." Sexuality is an important aspect of marriage. Sex was God's idea in the first place, and God also set clear boundaries within which one could enjoy sex to the maximum. One should not mistake the physical act of sex to be love.

When we develop a proper understanding of love and marriage, all of these aspects of love come with it, but those who have a distorted view of love will never fully enjoy any of the dimensions of love. Within the context of marriage, one can fully enjoy romantic feeling and sex. Genuine love grows with time and within a committed relationship.

Infatuation	Love
Fall in love suddenly	Grows with time
Deepens little with time	Always deepening
Up and down emotionally	Consistent
In love with love	In love with a person
Break up at slightest irritation	Does not panic when problems arise
Emphasizes external beauty and looks	Emphasizes character
Wants to get (selfish)	Wants to give (selfless)
Based on feelings	Self-controlled
Shows emotions	Shows devotion
Physical	Spiritual
Wants sex now	Willing to wait for sex within marriage
Focuses on the performance of the other person	Provides unconditional acceptance of the other person
May feel this way toward more than one person	Feels this way towards one and only one
Has idealized image of the person	Has a realistic view of others' strength and weakness
Avoids problems	Works through problems
Temporary	Permanent

What Love Is: Four Kinds

To understand what really love is we turn to the Bible. The New Testament was written in Greek, a rich language which has four different words that describe four different types of love. The first word *storge* means affection, a fondness toward family members. It is the love for family. It even describes the love that members of the animal kingdom have for their offspring. This word is most often used in referring to the love parents have for their children. Another word, *philia*, is used to describe the love that binds two friends together. It is the brotherly love from which we get the word Philadelphia–*the city of brotherly love*. Then there is *eros*, meaning sexual love, from which we get the word erotic. This is the physical aspect of love between man and woman. Finally there is *agape*, meaning unconditional love and points to divine, selfless and sacrificial love toward an undeserving other. This is the highest form of love and most often used to express God's love toward humankind in the Bible.

All four kinds of love show up in marriage. Within the context of marriage there is tenderness, companionship, sexual union and unconditional giving. No marriage can

> ### 15 Characteristics of Love
> *Love is patient, love is kind. It does not envy, it does not boast, it is not proud. It is not rude, it is not self-seeking, it is not easily angered, it keeps no record of wrongs. Love does not delight in evil but rejoices with the truth. It always protects, always trusts, always hopes, always perseveres. Love never fails.*
> – Paul (1 Corinthians 13:4–8)

be sustained by any one of them alone and nor should it be starved of any one of them. Moreover, agape love brings divine traits into the human relationship and is a powerful force towards the fulfillment and longevity of the marriage.

Love is action. To find out if you really love someone or if someone really loves you, substitute your name for **love** in the passage of 1 Corinthians 13:4–8. Then it would read as "Sam is patient (towards Mary). Sam is kind (towards Mary). Sam does not envy, does not boast and is not proud. Sam is not self-seeking. . .and so on."

The sacrificial, unconditional, agape love doesn't keep score. It doesn't matter how your spouse responds; if you want to love like Jesus loves, you have to put yourself aside. Agape is a love that gives, a love that does not demand or hold onto rights, but has the good of the other at heart. Agape is not dependent on any lovable qualities that the object of love possesses. Agape is the love that brings forth caring regardless of circumstance. It is considered as the greatest of loves and seen as distinctive Christian virtue.

Waiting for Love: Life on Hold

Nobody wants to wait for anything these days. We live in an instant world—instant coffee, cellular phones and credit cards. Emails are too slow that we communicate on instant messengers and texting. Instant gratification is a way of life. Waiting is a lost art. The same attitude spills into relationships as well for some as they move in and out of relationships.

However, many singles live waiting for Mr. Right (or Ms. Right) to rescue them from their plight. These singles are afraid to make any move. Waiting is harder now than ever before. Others rush into relationships without much consideration. With every passing month and year, it only gets more difficult. With fewer fish in the pool, no one seem to bite on your bate anymore. A friend's father once advised me, "If you don't catch one early, you lose out. It is like a triangle. At the base, you are still young, and there are many more choices for you. As you grow older, options dwindle."

When I (Mary) turned 23, my parents thought it was time for me to think about marriage. They started looking for suitable alliances for me, but I wasn't ready for marriage or interested in any conversation on the topic. Nothing much really happened. I was convinced that right person will come at the right time. When I reached 25, I waited for Mr. Right, but no one showed up. I immersed myself into research and my doctoral studies. One more year passed by and prince charming was not in sight. The years rolled on. I turned 28 and 29 and even 30. Finally, I met Sam when I was 31. Now when I look back, I realized I was not ready for marriage. I was fearful and selfish. We both tend to think even if we had met each other earlier, we would not have chosen each other and even if we had gotten married, we would have been miserable in our marriage. Each of us needed to change.

My (Sam) story is also somewhat similar. Soon after finishing engineering school, my parents brought few marriage alliances that had come to them and began hinting about getting married. I conveniently brushed it aside, saying my older brother should get married first. Instead I began pouring myself into a demanding career and graduate school. A quick rise in the corporate ladder and many career opportunities kept me from pursuing any relationship. At one point when I was 29, my parents began to worry

When there is love in a marriage, there is harmony in the home; when there is harmony in the home, there is contentment in the community; when there is contentment in the community, there is prosperity in the nation; when there is prosperity in the nation, there is peace in the world.
– Chinese Proverb

and brought many marriage proposals. I was getting so annoyed that I started avoiding them, and once I even told my parents that "I am wedded to my job, and I do not have any time to settle down in life."

Waiting is very hard. Nobody seems to understand your predicament. There is no help or support within your reach. Though waiting gets harder with each passing day, waiting for the right person is worth the wait. It is better to wait and get married to the right person than get struck with a wrong person and trying to make it right.

Waiting is harder for women in most communities. During my (Mary) waiting period, women were considered too old for marriage when they reached 27, parents suffer tremendous pressure from the society to get their daughters married off, which they tend to pass on to the young women. It is very hard for parents with unmarried daughters to meet their peers whose daughters are married well and even have grandchildren. Parents avoid community and religious gatherings in order to escape from their sense of failure and communal shame. Many parents succumb to such pressure and force children to get married against their will.

Working on Self: Being Mr. Right (Ms. Right)

Someone said, "if you want a princess, you've got to be a prince charming, and if you are looking for a prince charming to come riding to you on a horse, you've got to be a princess." For too long, our culture had a wrong emphasis when it comes to getting married by focusing on the process of finding the life partner. We somehow believe that finding the perfect match will lead to a perfect marriage.

> *Love does not consist in gazing at each other, but in looking in the same direction.*
> – Antoine de Saint

Instead of being preoccupied with finding "the right one" by having your profile on every matrimonial website or other matchmaking means, singles must focus on being the right person. They should take time to know who they really are and what they want in life and a relationship. They should focus on developing their strengths and healing from personal and relational wounds from the past, before entering into a serious relationship or marriage. What you bring to the table of marriage is crucial to what will become of your marriage.

We believe soul mates are not found, but are formed over a period of time with intentional investment into the relationship. Many get married and try to change their partner according to their preconceptions or expectations. Any attempts to force-fit the other into a predetermined mold is destructive to all parties involved.

None of us can change anyone else. All that we can do is to change ourselves, being committed to work at our own end and being a better person in the marriage.

Singles become so busy looking outside that they spend very little looking inside. They are so consumed with the process and the task of finding the other that they lose themselves. They must take their eyes off from finding a partner to know what kind of partner they will be in a marriage and try to improve what they will bring into the marriage. You will find a mate when you stop looking and take this time to learn all you can about yourself. Some think love conquers all. Nobody gets married with the intention of getting divorced. They hope their feeling will see them through. But this wishful thinking often leads to heartbreak. Experience shows that you can love someone deeply and still opt to divorce.

> *Everything that I understand, I understand only because I love.*
> *– Leo Tolstoy*

We all long to love and to be loved. There exists an innate need for love in all of us. Finding true and faithful love can be life transforming. But true love comes in sheep's clothing and many have been deceived by counterfeit love. Love is more of a choice than a feeling. Good marriages do not "just happen." It takes a great deal of hard work. It is less about finding the perfect person or pretending to be one. It is more about being the right person. My mate is not a solution for all my woes, nor can I change the other person to fulfill my selfish needs.

Love flourishes when couples work on their relationship. Unless both partners give instead of take, their love will die of malnutrition. People who do not know how to deal with the rough spots of marriage will not be able to keep loving feelings alive in marriage. The more we give and commit to a relationship, the deeper our love is and more satisfying the marriage will be. Marriage is a call to serve your spouse, even if it costs you dearly. That's true love!

Exercise-1: Personal Inventory

1. Personal

	Yours	Fiancé(e)
Name		
Date of Birth		
Nickname/Other Name: (Discuss its origin and why you were called so)		
Highest Education		
Occupation		

2. Parents

List the following details regarding your parents

	Father	Mother
Name		
Education		
Occupation		
Age		
Race/Caste		
Family Name		
Place or Origin		
Socio-economic status		

3. Home environment
Discuss your earliest memories of your home.

On a scale of 1–5 (1 =low, 5=high) how close are you to your parents?
Father _____ Mother_____

How would you describe the emotional environment of your home?

What three phrases would describe your growing up years? Why?

4. Siblings
List your siblings and discuss your relationship with them

Name	Gender	Age	Relational Closeness Scale of 1–5 (1-low, 5=high)

5. Education

List the institutions you attended and share some distinct memories about those stages of life

Pre-school

Elementary

Middle School

High School

College

Post College Education/Training

6. Work history

List all employments including part-time, summer and college jobs. Discuss what you found fulfilling and frustrating at each of those jobs

7. Friends

List all of your close friends at different life stages and identify at least one quality that marked your friendship

8. Medical history

List major health challenges you have had and how it has affected you

2

Choice Matters

Discerning the Most Important Decision in Life

The key to healthy marriage is to keep your eyes wide open before you wed and half-closed thereafter. (Unknown)

The lot is cast into the lap, but its every decision is from the LORD (Proverbs 16:33)

"I think I made a big mistake," texted Raj over his Blackberry to me, "When can I talk with you? Very urgent!"

Raj was married to Rani for little over a year. They had an arranged marriage. Their parents worked in the same company and the families had several common friends. They lived in different parts of the same city and hailed from a similar caste and faith backgrounds. Both were college graduates and had begun professional careers a couple of years ago.

When I called him back he admitted, "I think I got married to the wrong person."

"What happened? Why do you think so?" I asked.

"If I had married to the 'right' person—the one I was supposed to be with, I would not have all these problems. I think I came under pressure and got married to the wrong person."

Many young people have asked us over many years—"Is there one and only one person out there that I should marry? How do I know for sure he is the man for me? Is she is the one for me? How can I ever know that two of us make a great couple? How do I find that person? What if I missed God's best, will I be forced for the second best? etc."

Undoubtedly choosing whom to marry is one of the most weighty decisions we will make in life. Doubts are common and they trouble us greatly as we are in the process of making this decision. Whether you have already made that decision or only beginning to seriously consider a relationship, we want to guide you about the decision-making process when it comes to relationship so that you will not be in Raj's shoes.

People wrongly believe they have a "right" to a happy marriage, and therefore feel they have a "right" to divorce someone if things are not going as they want them to. It is also wrong to think there is one person out there who is the only one you can marry, as if God has taken one soul, split it in two, and put each part into two human beings who now spend their life longing for each other, and if not found, end up always having this unfulfilled longing.

Mate Selection: Choosing Wisely

We all make several decisions every day. What to wear, what to eat, what to do, whom to call or chat. We also make more long-term decisions, like choosing friends, where to live, financial, careers we pursue. Some are routine decisions without any long-term consequences, while others bear on us daily for a long time to come. Some do not cost a penny, while for others we pay for dearly. For every action, there is a reaction, likewise for every decision there are consequences. Some are insignificant, others will hound us for rest of our lives.

If you are still single and reading this book, we encourage you recognize the weight of the decision before you. This one decision has more to do with the quality of your future marriage than anything else we could do thereafter. The strength, stability and depth of marriage are greatly affected by individuals involved and what they bring to the table.

If you are already in a committed relationship or engaged to be married soon, we want to reflect on why you chose each other. What were the filters that you sieved your mate through? It is important to be absolutely sure of why you chose this person and the stages of coming to that conclusion. Your signs of confirmation, guidance in this journey, and hearing each other's story can greatly enrich your relationship.

This one decision is something that you cannot revisit or change your mind afterward. If you are unhappy with your job, you could change it. You could change your field of expertise. You can move to new town. We have gotten used to constantly changing culture and bring the same attitude into marriage. I will get married and try it for a while, if it works out then it is fine; or else will try it with someone else. This trial and error approach does not work in relationships.

> *Success in marriage is much more than finding the right person. It is a matter of being the right person!*

There has been a lot of confusion over the mode of mate selection. Some fall madly in love with each other, whether it was love at first sight or several sights. Some go the traditional way of arranged marriage. They feature their profiles on matrimonial and social networking websites. Some have grown up in homes where parents did not allow them to date. Generally singles must have gone by a combination of all of the above. If you are still single, we would encourage you to explore all avenues for meeting your potential mate. If you are already in a committed relationship or engaged, take time to share with each other about your reflection on the mate selection process and what did not work for you and what worked and why.

Looking for Love: Hard to Find and Decide

The challenge of finding a life-partner is harder than ever. We disagree with what some experts suggest "don't look for love, let love find you." Finding a lifemate is an active process. Don't expect someone to drop your future mate in your lap on a fine morning or evening for that matter. You must know who you are, what you are looking for, what you want in life and where you are headed in life. Knowing these would greatly help the process of searching for love.

The question is not simply where and how do we meet potential mates, but several new factors have been thrown into the equation of finding a mate which never existed for our parents or grandparents. They include like similar attitudes, economics, socio-cultural aspects (assimilation), psychological outlooks, education, relationship skills, life mission, spirituality, etc. Filtering anyone through this grid and being sure of what you are getting into is quite tricky.

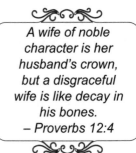

> A wife of noble character is her husband's crown, but a disgraceful wife is like decay in his bones.
> – Proverbs 12:4

There are numerous ways of finding a mate. Modes of mate selection have been diversified as arranged or referred, love, dating, online, speed-dating, advertisements on internet, newspaper, magazines, print media, meeting at social clubs, schools, colleges, community or religious gatherings, social networking etc. There is no one process that is superior over the other. Sometimes multiple processes of finding a mate could be pursued in parallel. There are also other process that happens some of which are unethical or immoral or dangerous or illegal.

Moreover, the role of matchmakers, community, family members and religious leaders are now being severely curtailed.

Most marriageable singles live independently, at least in terms of their aspirations or emotional longings and are more influenced by their peers, media, culture and personal spirituality. The weight of the decision also heavily lies on the singles themselves in some sections of the society. The fear of seeing broken marriages among their contemporaries makes the job of finding love really difficult.

Arranged Marriages: Old–New Ways

Traditionally in India, parents and extended family took the primarily responsibility to arrange the marriages of their children. When children come of age, which can mean a different thing to different people and has evolved over time, parents actively seek potential mates for their children. A century ago, it meant reaching puberty for women and entry into farm work for men. After Indian independence women were encouraged to pursue education, parents waited till women finished their schooling and looked for educated men. In the last few decades, college education was important milestone for entry into the marriage market.

In communitarian societies like that of India, where people knew a lot of other people, marriage alliances were made between distant relatives, acquaintances or neighbors. In most arranged marriages, the parents of the boy and girl would meet and agree on the conditions of their marriage, which included payment of dowry by the bride's father to the groom's father. This was a way of giving an inheritance to the daughter, as the daughter had no rights to the agricultural land. In some cases, the bride and groom see each other for the first time on the day of their wedding. This was a common practice for many of our parent's generations and before. This is still practiced among some sections of the society and in rural communities.

Some of the factors considered in an arranged marriages were a thorough research on family history, pedigree, character, values, status in society, wealth, caste, religion, mental health, physical features, fairness, beauty, ability of the "boy" to provide for the family, etc. before the alliances were made. Parents would make an inquiry through word of mouth on the potential candidate. Only after satisfactory findings would negotiations begin, akin to settling on a job in today's market. There was no question of divorce ever. The woman had to learn to adjust to the husband and his extended family and be subservient to her husband. As the marriage years progressed, the wife had increased responsibility and power in the household.

In recent years, parents seek potential mates for their children, but children make the decision whether to proceed with the proposal brought by the parents. The advantage of this mode is that there is no pressure on the children to find a mate for themselves until the time of decision making. A lot of research on the parent's proposal is done and the information is available to the child. Inquiries are being made to ensure the candidate is genuine, of good character and has a good job. After the boy and girl agree initially to pursue each other, they may talk over the phone or exchange e-mails, but have limited meeting opportunity before deciding to get married. The disadvantage of this mode is that it is hard to find all facts about a potential candidate and their carefully hidden private lives these days.

Love Marriages: Falling Head Over Heels

With the dispersion of people all around the world and loosening of familial bonds, parents find themselves helpless in their responsibility to find suitable mate for their children. Moreover, younger generations are more aware of their expectations, assertive and involved in the mate selection process. In addition, there is a growing cultural gap between parents and children, and they don't see eye to eye. Parents and children have different sets of values and criteria for mate selection.

In many cases, parents are not aware of their children's marital aspirations and leave it the children to take a lead. So a boy meets a girl or vice versa, they fall in love or become friends or date and get to know each other before they decide to get married. The adverse side of this is that these days the boy does not commit to marriage but dates endlessly, and the girl is eager to get married as she is getting along in years and would like to have children. It could be the other way where the girl is afraid to commit to marriage. Also, boundaries on emotional and sexual purity are broken with no marriage in sight. This also leads to live-in relationships.

People meet their mates in variety of different settings— school, neighborhood park, shopping malls, colleges, social clubs, community events, religious places, or singles gathering. The old days of marrying your childhood sweetheart or meeting someone at college and get married soon after graduation, isn't the way to go these days. People are in college longer, working through many jobs and trying to pay up their college

> *You may inherit all you own from your parents, but a sensible wife is a gift from the LORD.*
> – Proverbs 19:14 CEV

debt. The place of meeting your mate has shifted from school to college to now workplace or on the ubiquitous internet.

With the rise of individualism and young people wanting "to know" their future spouse, there aren't many traditional matchmakers. Most Indian newspapers and web portals still carry matrimonial advertisements for bride and groom seekers. But the growing trend is young people advertizing for themselves. Social and professional groups have helped many find their life partners.

Young adults in most societies are postponing marriage. They are staying single as they finish up their studies and try their hands in couple of different work environments. Some wait well into their thirties, which was unheard of in the Indian society in the past. Clearly, there are more choices open to women now than in decades past. Women are pursuing more studies than men and staying in college longer. Women are also financially independent and are self-supported these days. Many career women who no longer live with their parents feel less pressure to get married. They also have greater say in matters of choosing their life partners. As a result, they are less likely to run into their potential mates of their own.

Then, there are some other noteworthy social trends—speed dating, online matrimonial, long distance relationships, cohabitation, and same-sex relationship, all of which have undermined the sanctity and real meaning of marriage. Studies have proven that living together before marriage significantly reduces the success and longevity of the relationship.

Finding your mate is an active process. Waiting for someone to show up at your door will not yield results. If you are looking for a job, you do not just apply to one job and wait, but you research and spend much time and energy to call, e-mail and network until you find several suitable openings. How much more we are to search if we looking for a mate and how much more important decision is it than finding a job? Ask, it shall be given, seek and ye shall find and knock until the door opens. Be persistent. Don't be shy, tell the people around you that you are looking and what you are looking for. If you are shy, find a trusted friend or relative to help you with your search. Be willing to take calculated risk.

Virtual Love: Online Relationships

In recent years, there has been a plethora of internet dating and matrimonial sites on the web. It would range from posting marriage classified to a database of online profiles to psychological analysis and matching. They are grouped along the lines of age, language, caste, region and religion. Although a boon to singles, many internet-aided marriages have crashed prematurely.

The internet can open a world of potential partners you would probably never meet through traditional means. The do-it yourself matchmaking sites, based on those who share a faith, language, career, geographical location, immigration status or hobby, millions of potential suitors can be found. Virtually all these sites offer an opportunity to screen user profiles, while insuring anonymity for both parties. Anonymity does not mean the same as security, however. While some sites require personal references or an interview before allowing you to register, most sites rely on the integrity of the users. This creates a golden opportunity for a con-artist to log in and pretend to be someone he/she is not. Individuals who are less than satisfied with their own self are quick to reinvent a "new and improved" internet persona!

Having a larger pool to fish from does not make the process of finding love any easier. Advanced search technology or obscurity of the web cannot guarantee lasting love. The fictitious profiles create another complex layer to work through in getting to know your future spouse and come in the way of building a strong marriage. Despite its potential for abuse, online dating has helped thousands of single men and women initiate relationships. The best way to make internet dating work for you is to use it as a tool for introductions, rather than as a medium for conducting an extended online relationship. We have seen that ease with which a relationship begins also falls apart just as quickly.

The best way to start is by looking for potential mates within an easy to travel radius of your home. Simply exchange some innocuous information about each other and arrange to meet relatively soon after your initial online connection. But it is not a good idea to proceed with actual "dating" or relationship development over the internet. You need face-to-face interaction to determine if you are compatible and equally important, if you are physically attracted to each other. Do not be fooled by profile photos or self-descriptions.

It is tragic to learn that many build an emotionally intimate friendship with charming profiles and later discover that his/her personality, character or appearance are not what you bargained for. And when the two of you finally come face to face, you may not be able to adjust to the way the flesh and blood version differs from the fantasy you envisioned. Remember marriage is lived out in real world, not virtual. The "new and improved" online you, under a fictitious name, are a very wrong way to initiate or build a strong relationship. Starting and pursuing a relationship on a wrong note cannot be undone. They continue to live a lie for rest of their married lives.

Do not make up your mind based on online profiles. Filter through your grid of important pre-determined criteria. Ask for references and give references that both can approach to know about the other. Get the permission of references to give out their contact information. Meet in person as soon as possible and try to make the first meeting in group setting with family, friends or colleagues on a business trip. Be brutally honest about yourself and avoid any cover ups. Develop a strong sense of discernment. Of course, do not give your address, personal or financial information. Avoid divulging too much information about self virtually. Trust your instincts. If a person seems too weird or scary, or if you sense that you might be in danger, listen to the little voice inside you. It is better to be safe than sorry.

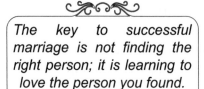

The key to successful marriage is not finding the right person; it is learning to love the person you found.

God's Will: Divine Perspective

Does God have a specific will concerning whom one should marry? If yes, how do you find that out? Does God overwrite my choice in any case? Why should I be responsible if it does not work out? Does it matter at all? Some fear that they might go out of the will of God or miss out "on God's very best." Many believe that there is only one person whom the Lord has selected for each Christian, and it is up to each Christian to find that person.

After matching all the characteristics and passing all the compatibility tests or even before considering a mate, one needs to be in prayer specifically relating to your particular situation. It would also be good to rope family and friends to pray for you. Since this is the second most important decision going to be made in your life, it is also important to be in prayer regarding their marriage partner and their marriage for years before. When I (Sam) was 16 years old, one of my Indian "uncles" asked me to pray for my life partner. Of course, I was quite embarrassed because nobody talked about marriage that early in life back then. I began to pray secretly and prayed for a Proverb 31 wife. Years later, I am only surprised how God has answered all those prayers in Mary. It was true of me (Mary) too. Many of the prayers I uttered as a single woman came fulfilled in Sam. Be careful what you pray!

The next step in seeking divine guidance is being plugged in the Scripture. When we abide in the living Word, God will determine your steps and thoughts. Of course, you will not find the name of your spouse or 'thou shall marry so and so' in the Bible. My (Sam) case was more of exception. When I was considering a relationship with Mary, Bible spoke to me literally, "Do not be afraid to take Mary as your wife!" Believe me there is a verse like that in the Bible. Check it out Matthew 1:20. The original context of the verse is an angel speaking to Joseph, the earthly father of Jesus, telling him not to divorce Mary because of premarital conception, but to marry her. The rest of the verse was not true in our case!

Seek godly counsel from men and women whom you trust. God's will becomes evident to us through the advices and inputs from older brothers and sisters. Choose someone, preferably someone older or a trusted friend, who has your best interest in mind and knows you quite well. This person must be spiritually mature, wise and should be wise in matters of relationships.

The next step would be to discern circumstantial evidence. If you are in perfect alignment with the will of God concerning your marriage, you will see many things falling in place. Some of it would be beyond any easy explanation and absolutely supernatural. You need eyes and a heart to see and discern these signs. Let us also caution you to reading too much into circumstances around you. Remember this will never be a primary sign on which you should decide whom to marry, but a supportive case to what was already revealed will of God for your life.

Discerning God's will requires that you are continually being, saying, living and doing God's will. You are in his word, in prayer and in a vibrant relationship with God. Every step, small or big, taken is lived for God's purpose and for his glory. Seek ye first the kingdom of God and all these things (including a mate) will be added unto you. Seek to hear God and fulfill his greater purposes for your life. God desires to reveal his plans concerning your life, including choosing your lifemate.

Choosing God: Eternal Difference

Divine guidance cannot be considered by itself apart from our personal relationship with God. Many desire the gifts but not the giver. If we long for guidance but do not thirst for God himself, we might not obtain the guidance we seek.

Even though we have been talking about how we go about choosing our life partners, there is another choice we all have to make in life which profoundly impacts our choice of a mate. This may be the most important and long lasting decision we would ever make. This decision concerns to which god do I offer my allegiance and life. There are many gods out there competing for our adherence and a variety of claims and counterclaims.

We both are followers of Jesus Christ and believe that he loved each of us enough to die in our place for our sins. His earthly life and teachings provide hope for the world. Having a personal relationship with the living God of the universe is foundational to pursuing and building a lasting and fulfilling marriage.

Will you refuse to accept his gracious free offer of salvation? Acknowledge that you are a sinner and in need of savior. Recognize that Jesus Christ had died for your sins and accept his pardon for your sins. Receive him into your life and ensure you will spend eternity with him. I hope you will stop and think afresh about the claims of Jesus and choose to have a relationship with him.

Besides the decision to follow Jesus Christ, whom you choose to marry, perhaps is the most important decision you will ever make. Choosing to follow Christ will secure your eternity, while whom you choose to marry impinges on rest of your earthly life. It has far-reaching implications, beyond yourself than anything else you have to decide ever. It affects not only two people involved, but their respective parents and siblings, extended families and even future generations. So choose wisely.

Exercise-2: Relationship Readiness

Are you ready for a relationship? Check all that apply

[ ] I feel lonely.

[ ] My parents and relatives are putting a lot a pressure on me to get married.

[ ] I am looking for companionship.

[ ] I have come of age and think this is the next stage of life.

[ ] All my friends are married.

[ ] Some dowry money will really help me financially now.

[ ] I need someone to talk to.

[ ] I long for romance.

[ ] I think my biological clock is ticking.

[ ] I am ready for relational commitment.

[ ] I have brought closure to past relationships.

[ ] I want to share my life with someone.

[ ] Marriage will add to my status in the community.

[ ] I need someone who can clean the house and cook.

[ ] I want to have children.

[ ] I want someone to take care of my aging parents.

[ ] I need sexual fulfillment.

[ ] I just ended a relationship and I looking for a replacement.

[ ] I want to escape from my dysfunctional family situation.

[ ] I feel trapped in my current relationship.

Marriage Matters
Understanding What Marriage Really Is

Marriages are made in heaven. So are thunder and lightning!

I will betroth you to me forever; I will betroth you in righteousness and justice, in love and compassion. (Hosea 2:19)

"Why make a big deal about getting married?" asked my friend, Bobby, in the middle of a casual conversation. He went on to inform me about his girlfriend and their future plans.

"She is doing her final semester of graduate studies in the city. We studied in the same college before, and I was a year ahead of her. We love each other deeply. She is moving in with me by the end of this month," he paused to gauge my reaction.

"Who wants to get married these days? Is there anything wrong with living together as a couple?" he asked.

I was still processing what he shared and could not imagine how far he has digressed from the views he held a few years ago and the traditional family from which he hailed. While still recovering from the shock, I inquired, "Is she okay with that? How about your parents?"

"Absolutely. She is the one who suggested the idea!" he paused and continued, "Of course, our parents do not know about our decision yet. Shouldn't I decide what I do with my life and with whom I live? Why drag our old-fashioned parents into these decisions. But we hope to tell them sometime soon."Bobby continued, "Why waste all that money in a grand community-wide wedding party? Moreover, I have been saving up all of my money toward buying an apartment. We want to have a baby right away!" In his practical sense, he is completely unaware of the risk involved in his actions.

In a culture of growing promiscuity, cohabitation and same sex unions, people have no idea what marriage really means. With the rise of divorce and unhappy marriages everywhere, singles wonder why people make a big deal about getting married. The very concept of marriage is being redefined. All that we hear from popular culture or peers about marriage and family are so negative that dysfunctionality has become normative. For many it has become simply a set of rituals or a mere formality.

For some, having grown up in dysfunctional homes, they are disillusioned about the very idea of marriage. They reason, "Why suffer like my mother trapped in a bad marriage" or "Why bother with marriage when it could not ensure my father's presence in my life?" When they see their friend's marriages falling apart or those who are entrapped in a troubled marriage, they wonder why bother about getting married in the first place?

Many of the obstacles that wound and even cripple a marriage are a direct result of a faulty understanding of marriage. After constant bombardment of wrong ideas about marriage, we begin to believe those lies to be true. Developing a correct worldview is utmost critical in building a lasting and fulfilling marriage.

Wedding vs. Marriage
Many young singles and their parents are confused about difference between wedding and marriage. Some wrongly believe that a large dowry and an elaborate, lavish, community celebration will

determine happiness and longevity of a marriage. Some rich and famous people throw grand parties (even if it is outrageous) with the desire of making the big day the happiest day hoping that happiness will continue for the rest of their lives.

A wedding is a one-day event and marriage is a lifetime journey. Much more preparation is devoted for the one-day affair than a lifetime of marriage. If you are already engaged, you are most likely deeply entrenched deeply in planning for the details of the wedding. You want to make sure that every "i" is dotted and every "t" is crossed for the biggest day of your life. But are you preparing for what comes after the wedding day?

Often, we allocate resources more for a one-day wedding and leave the rest to chances. We remain naïve and wishfully think that marital relationship will automatically succeed. If you are wondering what could you probably do now to increase your chances at your marital happiness or ensure the health of your relationship, then you've got the right book in your hands. This book is NOT about planning a perfect wedding, but it will help you prepare for a lifetime of happiness and a fulfilling marriage. This might not be much help in getting the right "wedding bell" for your one-day celebration, instead this book is aimed at guiding you through open and honest communication about things that really matter in your marriage.

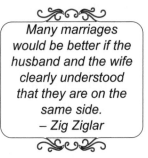

Many marriages would be better if the husband and the wife clearly understood that they are on the same side.
– Zig Ziglar

If you are not engaged yet, or pursuing (or hoping to) a relationship, this book and the worksheets will expose you to the reality of married life, and will provide keys to building strong relationships. You do not have to be married or even engaged to learn about marriage. In fact, why not get a head start on learning about what makes marriages work? Glean some understanding and culturally appropriate relational wisdom. It will undo some of the rough edges in your own life and help you to be a better person in your marriage. When you grow relationally wiser, you are more likely to meet a wiser people. When you are beaten up by life and have grown up relationally poor, you are more likely to meet or get attracted to someone just like you.

Ready for Marriage?

Having a successful marriage means more than FINDING the right person. It means BEING the right person. Before wedding we are other-focused—somehow find the other person and often after the wedding we become self-focused —how the other person must meet and satisfy my needs. It should be the other way around. Before the wedding, see what you bring to the table and after wedding see how you could serve your marriage.

For most people FINDING is the easier part. If you are still single, it may be hard for you to accept that, but it is true. You can go to places where single congregate or get some leads from family and friends. You can join clubs, pursue hobbies, enlist on a matrimonial websites or become active in religious or civic organizations. With some luck and wisdom, most of you will meet the one you consider Mr. or Ms. Right. But BEING the right person can be tougher. Are you easy to live with, generous, flexible, and willing to put your beloved's needs before your own? If you are still single after many years of intense searching, we do not want to downplay your hurdles in anyway. But we merely want to emphasize the harder challenge of BEING the right person which will continue into rest of your married life. The earlier you make this attitudinal adjustment, the better off your marriage will be.

So are you ready for this radically opposite view of marriage? How do you know you can commit the rest of your life to a person? Are you ready to commit and stick with the other person no matter what? Readiness for such radical commitment requires maturity. Are

> *Don't marry the person you think you can live with; marry only the individual you think you can't live without.*
> *– James C. Dobson*

you and your partner mature? Maturity means knowing who you are; knowing your talents, gifts, weaknesses, interests, the things you dislike, the values that you will not compromise, the preferences that you are willing to bend on, what you want out of life and marriage etc. If you are trying to cover up your weakness or not willing to work to improve them, you are not ready for intimate relationship like that of marriage, because within marriage our weaknesses stand exposed and they can never be covered up.

Out of this self-knowledge comes the possibility of giving oneself freely to your beloved. A proper understanding of self and marriage is the first step in preparing for a lasting marriage. In the rest of the book we want to walk you through this process and help you have a great start to your married life. Though much of it will be useful, you can never be fully ready for what lay ahead of you in married life. But having a right perspective and understanding on life and relationship are important preparation no matter what the future holds for you. So be prepared for little adventure!

Marriage: A Divine Idea

Marriage is not a man-made concept. Sociologists did not invent it nor did psychologists create this idea. The origin of marriage cannot be attributed to any group of people or any philosophies. It is not the brainchild of a culture or exclusively belong to any race or region of the world. Marriage is God's idea, not a man-made order at all. Marriage can be traced back to the Creator of the universe and hence marriage is a divine institution.

In order to understand what marriage really is, we have to go all the way back to the first marriage between Adam and Eve that God "conducted" in the garden of Eden. God sees the loneliness of Adam. Neither God nor the rest of the creation could fill his emptiness. Then God creates Eve out of a rib drawn from Adam's side. They were distinctively created male and female. When Adam wakes up to see Eve for the first time, he breaks out into love poetry. Love at first sight, I guess!

We could draw some inferences from the first marriage. Humans are uniquely created as relational being and we long for deep, abiding and intimate relationships. Marriage is the deepest of all relationship that we will ever have. Nothing else can come anywhere close to that. With the exception of a few who are called to a celibate lifestyle, I believe all are created to be married. God sees my void and calls that state as "not good." Then, God takes the initiative to bring a perfect match into our lives. God is a matchmaker and his matches work perfectly one hundred percent of the time. When God brings our future mates before us or leads us to discover for whom we are created for, we will know it intuitively. It is a spiritual revelation that we will discern perfectly when we are in tune with God and maintain close spiritual union with him.

While a good marriage can make happy people more fulfilled and may take away some loneliness, we should not need marriage to make life meaningful, give us worth, or be our sole source of meaning.

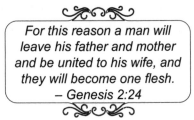

For this reason a man will leave his father and mother and be united to his wife, and they will become one flesh.
– Genesis 2:24

We should want to marry so that we can grow emotionally and spiritually and be able to give of ourselves to a spouse and children. If we are basically unhappy and don't feel that we have much to give, or if we mostly want to take, marriage only compounds our emotional problems and our dissatisfaction with life.

Marriage is intended to be a beautiful relationship described in pre-fall Genesis, in which the pain of loneliness is removed in the beautiful union of husband and wife, who work, play and love alongside one another without fear or shame. But since we are scarred by sin, we do experience pain, selfishness, fear, and shame. We hide parts of ourselves from one another. We hurt one another, sometimes deliberately, and we struggle for power and control. And all these things make it difficult to trust, be vulnerable, and to live in forgiveness. Some of us have a harder time than others, but successful marriages always require the best we have to offer along with heavy doses of forgiveness since our best will still be far from perfect.

Golden Rule of Marriage: Oneness

In the creation narrative, we find God establishing the first marriage saying, *For this reason a man will leave his father and mother and be united to his wife, and they will become one flesh* (Genesis 2:24). This commandment is known as the golden rule of marriage. In fact teaching on marriage by other biblical authors repeated this divine order (Matthew 19:5; Mark 10:7; and Paul's 1 Corinthians 6:16b and Ephesians 5:31).

Jesus is known for taking familiar Old Testament commandments and raising its implications to a whole new level. Whether it be prayer, murder or adultery, Jesus went to the heart of the issue. He knew the hypocrisy of keeping the law merely on the outside to impress people, when the heart was not involved. Jesus knew the superficiality that we all can get into so challenged status quo, meaningless traditions and vain authority figures of his day. He did not overthrow the commandments or the stipulations of the Old Testament but raised stake and gave fresh understanding to the commandments.

There is no more lovely, friendly and charming relationship, communion or company than a good marriage.
– Martin Luther

Except, in the case of one commandment, Jesus repeated the Old Testament mandate verbatim when it came to marriage. When the Pharisees asked Jesus if it was lawful for a man to divorce his wife, Jesus compared Moses' permissive law with God's creation order. He upheld the creation mandate over man-made provision and condemned the practice of writing a certificate of divorce. Jesus was overriding the interpretations of commandments and legal accommodations made by Jewish teachers, in order to account for hardness of human heart.

Marriage is an intimate relationship that Bible describes as "becoming one flesh." The word one is the same word used to describe God in Deuteronomy 6:4, which says, *"Hear, O Israel: the LORD our God , the LORD is one!"* (NKJV). The Hebrew word for one means "composite unity," as opposed to absolute unity. In the case of God, it is three who are one; in the case of marriage, two who are one. Relationship within the Trinity is the basis of all relationships, particularly the dynamic tension between unity and individuality of its members. There are two people with distinct personalities, gifts, names, and bodies. And yet marriage makes them one—an unbroken mysterious unity that transcends their individuality without obliterating it.

Marriage: Contract or Covenant?

In our business-driven world, marriage is sometimes wrongly seen as a contract. We live in a legalistic society. We get everything in writing and properly signed in the presence of a witness. Contracts and disclaimers are the way we make people or companies to live up to their claims.

> It is not your love that sustains the marriage, but from now on, the marriage that sustains your love.
> – Dietrich Bonhoeffer

They prevent us from escaping from our contractual obligations. For example, when signing for cellular phone service contract for a period of time, phones are given away free.

We bring the same mentality into marriage. Court marriages, pre-nuptial agreement, and wedding contracts force us to develop a similar outlook on marriage. We are more focused on what we can get from the other for our own happiness. This only leads to a tug-of-war resulting in much hurt, resentment, and anger, which eventually ends up in divorce.

In contract marriages, we agree to do something when other person will do something, much like of buying a car on a bank loan. I can enjoy its comfort, convenience and status, as long as I keep up my payments. When I default the contract, the bank has the legal right to repossess "my" car. When one party does not live up to the agreed upon contractual obligations, the other party can withdraw or take legal action.

Contracts are also time-bound and often contain an escape clause. It is motivated by extracting the most out of the other person, while important details are put in fine prints. We are sometimes tricked into agreements that we are not fully informed about. Lawyers craft legal contracts that average people cannot even understand, leaving them to fight the case alone.

Of course, in every marriage there are many practical arrangements or informal contracts when it comes to chores. For example, if one cooks the meal, the other cleans the dishes. One agrees to bathe the kids and the other take out the trash. However, the same mentality cannot be applied to fundamentals of marriage. A one hundred percent return policy in marriage (if I am not happy with my husband, I will come to my parent's place) is a bad idea. That is not the "leaving" that we talked about earlier.

Contrary to the characteristics of contract, marriage is a covenant. Covenant may be a new word for some of you and not commonly used in popular exchanges. It is an old English word with deep meaning. It is also a biblical word and God is presented as a covenant making and keeping God. Covenants are for the benefit of the other and are based on unconditional promises. A covenant relationship is permanent and lifelong. It is bound by life (meaning it is better to die than to break the covenant). It is based on steadfast love and open to confrontation and forgiveness. It causes personal growth and maturity. The depth of relationship and bond is unquestionably strong.

In the Bible, we find God establishing covenant with Noah (Genesis 6:18), Abraham (Genesis 17:3–8), Moses (Exodus 19:3–6), David (2 Samuel 7:12–29), and several prophets in the Old Testament. The relationship between the nation of Israel and God was covenantal. In the New Testament Jesus fulfilled the old covenant and instituted the new covenant (Matthew 26:28 or Luke

22:20). The apostle Paul developed and used the covenant concept as well (2 Corinthians 3:6, Galatians 3:15).

One of the poignant images of covenant is from the Abraham type of covenant. The actual covenant is found in Genesis 12:1–3, but the ceremonial ritual is recorded in Genesis 15. After God makes a promise to Abram, he offers an animal sacrifice. He cuts the animal into two halves and lays them opposite to each other. Later it the evening God appears to him and walks between the carcasses on the bloody trail, confirming his promise to Abram.

The story depicts the unconditional nature of covenant. The only time that both parties of a covenant would pass between the pieces of animal was when the fulfillment of the covenant was dependent upon both parties keeping commitments. Regarding the significance of God alone moving between the halves of the animal, it is to be noted that it is a smoking furnace and a flaming torch, representing God, not Abraham, which passed between the pieces. Such an act, it would seem, should be shared by both parties, but in this case it is doubtless to be explained by the fact that the covenant is principally a promise by God. He is the One who binds himself. God caused a sleep to fall upon Abraham so that he would not be able to pass between the two halves of the animal. Fulfillment of the covenant fell to God alone and was fulfilled at the sacrifice of his only begotten son—Jesus on the cross of Calvary. Christ's death points to the covenant keeping nature of God and how seriously he took the promise he took.

Why Marriage: Real Motivation

Before we get any further, let me ask you one basic question— why do you want to get married? What are the real reasons behind your decision to formally be husband and wife? What would your rationale for tying the knot? Do you have any strong motives for getting married?

Many enter into wedlock with very wrong or ulterior motives. For some it is companionship, while for others it is sexual union.

Some think they have "come of age" and marriage is the next stage in life. Others crumble under parental pressure and get married in order to get their parents off their back. When all of your friends are already married and having kids, you may feel an inner urge to settle down like everybody else. Some get married to escape from a defective home environment, while others try to fill their loneliness in life.

If you try to find intimacy with another person before achieving a sense of identity of your own, all of your relationships become an attempt to complete yourself. You will try to manipulate the other person in order that they fit into your ideals. You will use and even abuse the other person to satisfy your own needs, which is a very wrong motive to pursue relationship.

Seven Wrong Reasons to Marry
1. To Get out of your parent's house.
2. No one better will ask me to marry him/her.
3. High time to get married.
4. Being abused, blackmailed or forced to do things you don't want to do by your partner.
5. If either of you are dependent on drugs, alcohol or other things.
6. If you and your partner have major issues that you are avoiding because it might upset your relationship like pregnancy, finances, money, school/career etc.
7. Marriage is next logical step.

When we enter into romantic relationships looking to complete our identity, the relationship becomes a very selfish thing that will slowly destroy both of God's masterpieces involved. For a relationship to really work, it has to be built on the principle of give and take. Too many relationships tend to be more take than give, which leaves both parties empty, angry and looking elsewhere to be filled again. This leads to a destructive pattern that gets established as you go from person to person and never actually find what you are looking for.

Exercise-3: View of Marriage

This exercise helps to understand how other marriages have shaped your view of marriage. Make a list of the marriages in your circle of acquaintances. For example, parents, siblings, close friends, colleagues, extended family, etc.

List out at least three positive and negative traits of each of those marriages. Discuss what traits are worth emulating and how you would incorporate it within your own marriage. Also discuss what traits you would avoid and how.

No	Marriage	Qualities that I admire	Qualities that I dislike
1		1.	1.
		2.	2.
		3.	3.
2		1.	1.
		2.	2.
		3.	3.
3		1.	1.
		2.	2.
		3.	3.
4		1.	1.
		2.	2.
		3.	3.
5		1.	1.
		2.	2.
		3.	3.
6		1.	1.
		2.	2.
		3.	3.
7		1.	1.
		2.	2.
		3.	3.

Life Matters
Mapping Your Journey

The hardest thing about examining your life is getting started. (Socrates)

"I have come that you may have life, life to the fullest." (John 10:10)

Naveen and Nimmy were made for each other. They had a dream wedding and all expense paid honeymoon. They were childhood sweethearts and seemed like a perfect match. She expected that they would enjoy walking hand in hand on the beautiful beach and have romantic candlelight dinners every evening over long intimate conversations.

But reality soon overtook her dreams. A month after the wedding, Naveen got a promotion, and he was expected to work long hours and travel overseas. He was excited about the opportunity and was keen on proving himself at this new assignment. But Nimmy stayed home alone in a new city where they had moved after the wedding away from friends or relatives and suddenly her dreams turned into a nightmare. Though she was the one who encouraged her husband to accept the promotion, she felt confused and disappointed. He felt caught between a demanding boss at work and crying wife at home. No matter how hard he tried, neither seemed to be happy.

All of us bring many expectations and unique life experiences into our marriage. Some good, some surprising and some unpleasant. We cannot selectively leave some things behind, even if we wanted to. We may think we have forgotten about them and dealt with them conclusively. Our experiences have shaped who we are now and will permanently become part of our marriage. Our present circumstances and daily decisions, our fears and expectations can seriously affect our marriage, more than we think it would.

Whether we like it or not our mates also will bring their past experiences, current circumstances and dreams about future life together into the marriage. Learning about each other's life journey and knowing how they can affect your life and your relationship with your future spouse is an important element in building a strong and healthy marriage. We should also prepare to embrace our mate completely and not let your discovery about the other person drive a wedge between both.

Sadly, in matters of pursuing relationship, most singles or newly married couples fail to realize the impact of what they bring to the table of marriage. They are so focused on the other and assume a perfect self or that is how we portray ourselves before others, we are blind to our own imperfections, which are glaringly obvious to our mates. So the wisest and best thing to do whether you are pursuing a relationship or engaged is to do self-examination; being brutally honest about yourself and seeing what you need to be a better person in the marriage. Many enter into marriage with an idea to change one's mate into one's ideal image. Instead of trying to get someone to fit our image, we can learn about and appreciate a partner for who he or she is.

A perfect marriage is not a result of two perfect people coming together, but two imperfect people coming together and allowing a perfect God work through them for his great purpose and to serve each other. When our partners do not match our ideal image, we try to fix them. The only person you can change is yourself. Be the change your want to see in your marriage. It is not about ***finding*** a perfect person, but ***being*** the best person you can be in the marriage.

Autobiography: Journeying Together

Immediately after our wedding, we went to Andaman Islands (known as the Indian Hawaii) for our honeymoon. I (Sam) was born on these islands. Before our wedding, we talked at great length about our childhood and upbringing and I ended up developing an autobiographical sketch of my life until that point in life. We went to the hospital where I was born, homes where I lived in and schools I attended. I was letting Mary enter into my life literally, reliving every stage of my life and letting her have a glimpse of my life experiences. Sharing some experiences were not easy, but it brought tremendous healing and intimacy into our relationship.

The longest journey of any person is journey inward.
– Dag Nammarskjold

If you were to make a film about your entire life and show it to your mate, what would it look like? Will it help your mate to see who and what has shaped you to be the person you are today? Can you be absolutely candid with yourself and reveal difficult experiences to your mate? See chapter 6 "Past Matters" on how to heal and recover from past negative experiences.

Mapping out the road of life require that you tell your story to each other. When we share our uphill climbs, dark valleys we've traveled through, bends along the roads, exits we took, and rivers we crossed, our mates get to see life experiences that shaped us. It provides a bird's eye view of major milestones in your life to your mate. It also helps you to understand yourself and how life circumstances and the world around you have fashioned you.

No matter how well you think you know each other or even if

you have grown up in the same town and went to the same school all your life, you will be surprised by how your autobiographical sketch can be so different. Being absolutely transparent about yourself also prevents keeping anything hidden from your mate, which will deepen intimacy in your marriage.

As you work through your autobiographical sketch, plan to record your place of birth, earliest memories of home, friends, tragedies, communities you were part of, favorite teachers, first job, church, spiritual experiences etc. Share some emotionally high and low points in your life, academic and career choices, and dating or marriage alliances. If your family relocated or migrated, include various cultural influences and assimilation patterns you see in yourself.

Know Thyself: Taking Stock of Life

We also bring our unique backgrounds, personalities, spiritualities, worldviews and tastes into our marriage. The way we think, act, feel and relate are products of who we uniquely identify. The better we understand ourselves and our mates, the better off we are in marriage. Learning about your mate will help

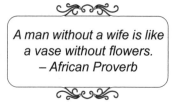

> A man without a wife is like a vase without flowers.
> – African Proverb

you know where one is coming from and why does one what one does.

While autobiography is chronologically ordered, the stock-taking is person-oriented and helps you to understand yourself better. It is aimed at helping the other enter the personal recesses of our lives. Letting them know who you really are and how you think and feel about various things of life. It will help you understand the personality type of your life partner and various preferences he/she may have.

We think we know ourselves pretty well, but marriage is such an intimate relationship that our mates will discover things about us that we are not even aware. Everything stands exposed within marriage and often our mates are X-ray machines, reading deep into the core of our being. There is no room to fake life and sooner or later your mate will know the real you. It is better to bare your souls to each other earlier in your relationship than to leave it to random discovery.

Though it may not be possible to understand ourselves fully or to use our self-knowledge act as a guide to all our future behaviors, introspection increases our self-awareness. Getting to know ourselves is all about knowing our own habits, morals, temperaments, and other aspects of human behavior that we struggle with on a daily basis. It provides a psychological maps giving indication of various tendencies from where all human behaviors stem.

Great Expectations: Too Great. . .Too Many

We all bring a set of expectation into our marriage. Some are obvious, and many are hidden deep within one's soul. Some expectations are never spoken about while others remain in our subconscious or unconscious self. Some clash the day after the wedding while others remain latent, like a volcano, only to erupt at the least expected time!

There is nothing wrong with having expectations. Everyone has them. Letting your partner know of your expectations and the rationale behind them can greatly strengthen your relationship. Let there be no surprise after the wedding and let your relationship flourish in an environment of transparency and trust. Also sharing how those expectations came to be and why they are so important to you would be immensely beneficial.

Most expectations find its origin in family, traditions, culture or faith. As we watch our parents' marriage, we absorb some silent imperatives about the roles of husbands and wives. Television shows, movies and books have undeniable influence on our expectations of marriage. During teen and young adult stages of life, our peers significantly shape our outlook on relationships. Previous friendships or romantic relationships will surely affect your expectations. Our cultural and religious affiliations mandate certain expectations on marital issues. Traditions practiced within our homes and community establishes its own set of expectations on us.

We tend to believe that our spouses will somehow meet all of our expectations. When they fail, couples blame each other and feel betrayed or cheated. We believe that in a perfect marriage our mate will intuitively know our deepest needs and heal our wounds. But no matter how perfect of a person your mate is, he/she cannot meet all of your expectations. Nonetheless, learning about each other's expectations sets realism and takes off the pressure of meeting the unexpressed needs of your mate.

> *Marriage is that relation between man and woman in which the independence is equal, the dependence mutual, and the obligation reciprocal.*

Expectations can include where we live, how many kids we will have, the role of the husband/wife, handling money, time spend at home, vacation, life goals, relationship with parents, faith affiliation, romance, frequency of sex, household chores, driving styles, cleanliness, and religious activities. No matter how thoroughly you analyze the expectations of your mate, be prepared to have some surprise discoveries of each other!

Having unrealistic expectations of marriage can bring a couple to the point of wanting to call it quits. Unrealistic expectations can lead to disillusionment in marriage. Expectations need to be verbalized with one another. A key to dealing with expectations is not to assume anything. Together you can fine tune your expectations so that neither of you are trying to live up to something that is impossible. Expectations also change over time, for example, when a family grows or relocates to a new city or have a desire for a roomier home may replace the wish for a new car or vacation.

Early in marriage, expectations seem less obvious to most couples. You expect very little, you feel great, and you are spending a lot of time trying to please each other. But as the relationship deepens, expectations change. And when you are not getting those needs met, suddenly your partner can do little that pleases you. Everything seems annoying or nagging. Every frustration just proves that your relationship is not right and is sapping your energy. You may start arguing and fighting, most of the time not about the real issues that are bothering you. Constant communication and spelling out your expectations is essential to maintaining a healthy and harmonious relationship. Remember, your mate cannot read your mind!

Fear Factor: Scary

All of us are scared of something or the other. Fears can paralyze us into inaction. We also bring our fears into our marriages. Examples are: "What if my marriage does not last?" or "Will I be a terrible father?" "I might get fired at job this year" "Fear of being alone or intimacy" etc. Some people marry because they're scared that no one else will marry them. Remember, it's better to be left on the shelf than spend your whole life in the wrong cupboard!

In addition to personal and relational fears, some might have fears or serious phobias. It could be heights, snakes, enclosed spaces etc. Some of it might be intense, irrational and persistent. Its effects could be debilitating and interfere with your marriage. Within a marriage, our fears stand exposed and a couple would be in a better place to face them together than individually.

Your fears may be influenced by many factors, including experiences of friends, previous relationships and media images. But one of the most powerful influences will be your family. As small children we learn about relationships by watching our parents. These messages often sink deep into our unconscious mind, waiting to pop up when we become wives or husbands ourselves. It's perfectly natural to have doubts and fears about getting married—it's one of the biggest decisions we make in our lives. But as long as you and your partner can openly share your feelings, support and reassure each other, chances are you're on the right track.

Facing your fears is important aspect of marital preparation. Honestly share your fears with your mate. Try to understand your mate's fears. Do not take them too lightly or try to find simplistic fixes. Being aware of each other's fears is the first step to facing them together. Talking of its origin and how long you have felt these fears can spark greater understanding and intimacy in your relationship.

Life Goals: Where Are You Headed?

Early in our courtship, Mary asked me a question, "Where do you see yourself in 25 years?" I fumbled something to impress her, but that question made me seriously think about my relationship with Mary on the long haul. I told her that I wanted

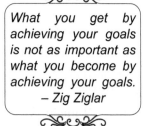

What you get by achieving your goals is not as important as what you become by achieving your goals.
– Zig Ziglar

to grow old with her and raise few kids, and shared my vision for helping families. It also made me think about legacy issues—what are we goingato leave behind or what will the world remember about us as a couple?

Sharing life goals is a tremendous tool for any couple headed toward the wedding aisle. As you dream your life together with your mate, it would be appropriate to reflect on how you see your future life. Life goals reveal a lot about a person. Aspirations and ambitions are a driving force in life that will impart to you priorities and visions about the future. Some may clearly articulate them and some may have great difficulty in seeing beyond present week, let alone five years!

Goal setting is a powerful process for thinking about your future together and for motivating yourself to turn this vision of the future into reality. The process of setting goals helps you to choose where you want to go in life. By knowing precisely what you want to achieve, you know where you have to concentrate your efforts. You will also quickly spot the distractions that would otherwise lure you from your course.

Goals bring focus. Having no goals is like going on a trip without a map. Where there is no destination or vision, most people tend to drift. Goals enable you to measure progress. It is impossible to measure how well you have performed if you have set no goals against which you measure your progress. Goals are motivating. When there is a target, we are more likely to get somewhere near it. Goals enhance self-esteem. Setting and achieving goals make people feel good about themselves. Goals increase commitment. When people have a vision of where they want to go, they tend to feel a greater sense of commitment than they would without having a vision. Goals motivate and increase effective teamwork.

Goals must be SMART—Specific, Measurable, Attainable, Realistic and Time-bound. Write down your goals and share it with your mate. Find synergy between your life goals and set some goals for your life together. Set realistic goals and avoid the temptation to impress your mate with ambitious life plans. Always articulate your goals as positive statement rather than negative statement. Try to include six areas for setting goals: education, career/financial, home/family, health, social and spiritual. Write out a personal mission statement and together work on marriage mission statement. "My" goals and "your" goals should converge into "our" goals, so that both marriage partners resources and leverages in achieving those goals.

Exercise-4a: Know Yourself

1. When do you feel inspired? When do you feel afraid? Sad?

2. Who or what makes you feel angry?

3. Who are the three most influential people in your life? How did they influence you?

4. What is it like being you? Describe how you feel about yourself physically, emotionally, spiritually?

5. What does God mean to you? How has faith or spirituality guided or hindered your life?

6. Who do you turn to for advice? Why?

7. Who are your closest friends? Why? Do you dislike anyone? Why?

8. How well do you articulate your thoughts?

9.   Describe yourself on a value scale: conservative, moderate, liberal.

10. What would like people to say about you at your funeral?

11. What is the most important thing in the world to you?

12. What is your dream job? What is your dream house/car?

13. Do you feel energized or drained in the company of others?

14. How do you usually get into trouble and how do get out of it?

15. If there were no constraints of time and money what would be the one thing you would like to do in life?

16. What makes you feel loved [appreciated/recognized/affirmed]?

17. If you had one day left to live, how would you live it?

18. What are some areas that you feel passionately?

19. What are your personal strong and weak points?

20. What's your favorite pastime?

21. What do you love to read, listen to or watch?

22. Describe your education and work experiences. Why did you choose this field of study or career?

23. What are your natural talents or spiritual gifts?

24. What is your definition of an ideal husband/wife?

25. What do you consider your major achievement in your life so far?

Exercise-4b: Personality Matrix

Take a blank sheet of paper and divide into four equal quadrants as shown below.

On the left column you list your positive and negative traits and values respectively. On the right side column you list both positive traits that you desire in your future mate and negative traits that you would avoid. Pick five to ten characteristics traits or values for each quadrant from sample list given below.

	Self	Future Mate
Positive		
Negative		

List of traits and values

Tall, handsome, beautiful, fair, friendly, kind, educated, charming, gracious, sense of humor, communicator, good listener, strong character, emotionally healthy, creative, patient, adventurous, attractive, tolerant, clean habits, loving, affectionate, industrious, smart, confident, intellectual, curious, unassuming, problem solver, organized, out-going, stylish, flexible, loyal, teachable, energetic, religious, spiritual, god-fearing, baptized, spirit filled, professional, social, optimistic, expressive, reserved, youthful, self-controlled, status, class, family background, pedigree, generous, responsible, passionate, family oriented, service oriented, graceful, grateful, kind, gentle, humble, truthful, leader, team player, ambitious, timeliness.

Arrogant, introvert, alcoholic, social drinker, drug user, depressed, dependent, angry, lazy, worrying, intolerant, childish, liar, cheat, irresponsible, petty, selfish, controlling, manipulative, fault finding, showy, status conscious, dowry seeker, ambitious, greedy, workaholic, disrespectful, obese, short, gambling, intrusive, rude, grudge, mean, denial, materialistic, consumerist, cynical, addiction, pessimistic, racist, chauvinist, tv addict, sports addict, judgmental, critical, hypocrite, shy, bad mouth, cheap, undependable, reckless, fanatical, argumentative, obsessive, aggressive, "I am always right," sloppy, unorganized, tardy, self-centered, narcissistic, weak, careless, jealous, proud.

Exercise-4c: Expectations

1. Identify expectations you have for your marriage and discuss it with your fiancé(e).

2. From where do think these expectations originate (family of origin, education, personality, culture, media, etc).

3. Why are these expectations important to you?

4. What would you do if your mate does not meet your expectations?

Professional/Social

5. How many hours will spend at work?

6. How often will work overtime or bring work home?

7. How much commute/travel will undertake for work?

8. Where do see your career in 5 years? 10 years?

9. How time and money would you spend for entertainment (television/movies/music/games/internet)?

10. What hobbies or pastime activities (gardening/reading/painting) will you pursue?

11. How often will you entertain friends at home?

12. How much time or money will you spend on friends?

13. How will you relate to same/opposite gender friends after marriage?

Marital roles

14. Who will prepare the meals?

15. What kind of food do you prefer to eat?

16. Who will clean the dishes? Who will make bed, clean floors/bathrooms? Who will do chores around the house?

17. Who will do the laundry, fold clothes, buy groceries, maintain the automobile, do house repairs, yard work, cleaning?

18. Who will dispose the trash?

19. How often will you have a meal together with family and how important is it to you? How often would you eat out?

20. How will you make decisions? What will you do when you are not in agreement?

Home

21. Where will you make your first home? Will you rent or buy?

22. Where will you go on vacation? How much would spend on your vacation?

23. Would you like to have a pet?

24. When will you have your first child? How many children would you like to have?

25. What would do if you have an unplanned pregnancy?

26. What would do if you cannot conceive?

27. What is your view on abortion, birth control?

28. How often do you expect to experience sexual intimacy?

29. How will we celebrate our birthdays, wedding anniversaries?

30. Where will you spend holidays (Thanksgiving/Christmas/Other)?

31. How often do you want to visit your parents?

32. What kind of cars would you like to drive?

33. What would do expect your standard of living to look like after 5 years of marriage?

Parents

34. How will your relationship with your parents change after marriage?

35. How will parents and in-laws be involved in your life and family?

36. What would you do if your parents or in-laws interfere?

37. Who are the relatives who will be involved in your family life?

38. How will you support your aging parents?

39. What could you do to honor your in-laws?

Finances

40. Who will be the financial provider?

41. Who will balance the checkbook and pay the bills?

42. Will you develop a home budget and stick to it?

43. How will you decide on major purchases?

44. What will you borrow money for?

45. When will you use credit cards?

46. How will your career or home income change when you have children?

Spiritual

47. What does spiritual leadership mean?

48. How much time will you take for family prayer? What will your family prayer look like?

49. What are your spiritual disciplines (prayer/fasting/Bible reading)?

50. Where will you go to church and how often?

51. How much money do you expect to give to church and other missionary or charitable causes?

52. What will your involvement in the church or community service look like?

5

Gender Matters
Knowing the Differences

"I'm returning the glasses I bought for my husband. He's still not seeing things my way." –Wife at an Eyeglass Store.

So God created man in his own image, in the image of God he created him; male and female he created them. (Genesis 1:27)

Rani lost her dad when she was barely six years old. Her mother raised Rani and her two sisters with help of her widowed grandmother. She grew up in an all women household. She had fond memories of her dad and adored him still.

Soon after Rani graduated from nursing school, her mom brought a marriage proposal that had come her way from a close friend. The young man, Raj lived in the same city and hails from the same local community. In fact, both had attended the same elementary school, but they did not really know each other back then. He had finished his bachelor's in economics and was working at an accounting firm.

Rani's mom had been worrying about her daughter's marriage and wanted her to get married at the earliest. This looked like a good proposal, and she was keen on marrying off her oldest daughter. But as Rani began to interact with Raj, she felt that he was not anything like her or anyone else she knew closely. They did not have any common interests and were having constant arguments. With the mounting misunderstandings, she began to doubt if he was the one for her and did not know how to communicate her fears to him or her mother.

As Rani began to describe her fear and confusion to a counselor friend of ours, it became evident that much of the problem arose from her lack of understanding of men in general. Raj was being a typical guy and Rani was disillusioned over the turn of events in her relationship with a man. Not having interacted with the male gender closely, she expected Raj to be more like her and did not know how to communicate with him.

Beyond stereotypical masculinity–femininity differences and culturally shaped differences between the sexes, gender issues really matter in intimate relationships like marriage. Men and women have different emotional needs and are often unaware of each other's needs. As we relate to others, we tend to give what we want or need. No matter how much you keep giving, a couple will feel unloved and distant from each other. Before the wedding bells, every couple must develop a deeper understanding of the battle of the sexes and have a strategy so that both can win. You must learn to embrace the uniqueness of your mate and celebrate the differences. Making the differences deepen your marriage is an indispensable task for all newlyweds.

In addition to inherent differences between the genders, biases and inequality further drives a wedge between men and women due to cultural preference for boys over girls in many male-dominated societies. Gender disparity is also accentuated by social status, educational achievements, cultural and religious beliefs. Deeply entrenched stereotypes on roles and overt interpretations of religious texts to subjugate women into subservience are commonly seen in many parts of the world. Reflecting on our own conceptions of gender issues and what has shaped our views will greatly enhance our relationship. Also, it is important to share your own understanding of gender differences and to develop a model of marriage where your differences will complement rather than clash.

Differences: Obvious and Ignorant

It is an obvious fact that men and women are not alike, even down to their DNAs. Some even claim that they come from different planets all together. Others have compared men to waffles and women to spaghetti, men like buffaloes and women like butterflies, etc. Analogies have been made with different vegetables and animals. The bottom line is: if you are married for any length of time or have grown up with an opposite gender sibling, you know this fact very well—men and women are different!

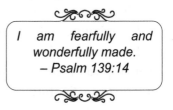

I am fearfully and wonderfully made.
– Psalm 139:14

If we take a closer look at human physiology, biological functions or psychological makeup, it confirms that we are dissimilar from each other. The obvious one is male and female anatomy. Men are generally bigger, stronger, have higher metabolism, lung capacity and sex drive. Women have larger stomachs, kidneys, livers and appendix. The skeletal structures and chromosomal makeup in every cell are different. Women have exclusive functions absent in men—menstruation, pregnancy and lactation.

Glands function differently in both sexes. Emotionally, we react differently. Women laugh and cry more readily, and they are more moody and unpredictable in their behavior (blame it on the hormones!). Men are often clueless about what is going on inside or how they really feel about anything. They are often crude and insensitive.

From cradle to grave, at every stage, men and women are

different. Women generally begin to crawl and walk before their male counterpart. They start talking earlier and never stop thereafter! From our brains to our toes we are fashioned distinctively. Men and women differ quite a bit in their tolerance for heat and cold. Men's brains are larger, but women's brains contain more brain cells. Our perspectives on issues are so dramatically divergent. It is estimated that women generally use between seventeen and twenty-five different items to get ready to go out (that explains why it takes longer to get dressed!). No wonder women are twice as likely as men to skip breakfast. Marital spats are common over who controls the thermostat or television remote. Since we are wired so differently at the core of our being, these differences hold possibility for persistent conflicts or developing deeper understanding and greater mutuality.

Of course, there are exceptions to all these generalizations of gender caricature and are not intended to advocate any particular gender stereotypes. As you learn to appreciate each other's differences, it will help you strengthen your relationship. Nevertheless, it would appropriate to dive further into male–female differences. To suggest that men and women are different is not to say that one is better than the other. Different does not mean superior or inferior, it simply means "not the same as." There is no value judgment in these generalizations. The sense of discovery and fulfillment we find in relating to people who are so different is part of what makes male–female relationship so exciting and challenging.

Inherited patterns from our parents also shape our gender roles and behaviors. Oftentimes, men and women behave like their fathers and mothers respectively. Some leave wet towels around the house, and others, after a long day's work sit in front of television watching favorite sporting event or skim through the evening news channels while ordering his wife to bring him hot cup of tea. Some women will choose to pursue careers because they came from homes of working moms, some other women who suffered neglect of a working mom, want to be home to care for their children. We bring into our marriages what we have seen in our parents' marriage.

Men and women differ in other ways as well. Our outlook on life, personality, and our senses of cleanliness or orderliness differs from each other. Men tend to think in boxes, and women are whole-brain thinkers. Men reason in compartments, and women think holistically. Women may say one thing but mean something else and men hear what they say and not what they mean. Before the wedding bells, we remain oblivious to our differences or may even be attracted by them. We know of a couple, Prakash and Priya. Prakash is generally a quiet guy and was an accountant by profession. Priya is a very expressive girl and was a school teacher by training. He worked with numbers and spreadsheets all the time, while she dealt with chatty elementary school kids. Before they got married, she was attracted to him for being a good listener and he loved her talkative nature. A few months after their wedding, they aired their complaints with us. She said that he does not talk much, and he said she talks all the time and never gives him a turn!

They were the same people, but saw the same characteristic differently before and after the wedding. What seemed to have attracted them to each other before was now repelling them from each other. What was a fascination had now turned into a frustration. They began to resent the same qualities that had drawn them to each other and why they wanted to get married to each other in the first place.

I (Mary) prefer a few close friends rather than many casual acquaintances. At social gatherings, I would settle to converse with at most two or three people. She believes in deep conversations and getting to a person. She talks less and listens to people intently and whatever she says is worth its weight in gold. I (Sam) on the other hand will want to shake hands with everyone under the roof. I believed in expanding my social network and getting to "know" people by knowing their names. I am a mile wide and an inch deep. While Mary is an inch wide and a mile deep!

His vs Hers: Worlds Apart

When it comes to gender difference, stereotypes abound. People portray how men and women think or behave based on their sex. It might be generalization and oversimplified view of people, nevertheless it is important to know gender–based difference that you and your mate bring into the marriage. Though masculinity and femininity are beyond standard caricature, there is wisdom in recognizing differences you both bring to the marriage.

Right from the birth announcement, boys and girls are said to be different in every culture. Parental pride differs, we deal with boys and girls distinctively, dresses and toys differ a great deal, societal perception (women stay at home, instead of pursuing a career outside of the home), economic disparity (women make less than men for the same job and responsibility). Many women feel they were not treated equally at home with other siblings. Mom and Dad had distinctive roles and children were encouraged to follow the same. Social rules of interaction, media and school system promotes messages about how we should look, think and act based on our gender. Yet, some of the following gender–based distinctions are unavoidable to observe when it comes to marriage.

Our culture has muddied the pool of gender issues in terms of equality and "women as good as men" talk. Some ask guys to get in touch with their "feminine self" and vice versa. It can be intensely exasperating trying to be something you are not. Instead of believing in the lie it is all the same and there exist no difference across gender lines, I suggest we understand gender difference and use them to help your relationship thrive. Some of the gender stereotypes might not even be true in your case and we suggest you learn about each others unique personality, weighing the challenges of accepting one another as he/she is.

Our brains are different. Our body structure is different. Our gland secretions are different. We see life and the world from completely different angles. We speak different languages. When you are in relationship, women assume men will do the same things women do when they love someone and men assume women will react the way a man would react when he loves someone. The battle of the sexes ensues from our misunderstanding of each other. Knowing we are different from each other frees us from feeling rejected and unappreciated. We also mature when we learn to accept our partner as they are.

Men generally tend to be objective and logically driven. They are goal oriented and tend to be problem solvers. Men are more inclined towards risky behavior and possess higher risk taking abilities. Men need their "caves" to retreat into from time to time and women must understand that a man's healthy need to withdraw can greatly enhance their relationship. Give him the space he needs and he is sure to come out of it. Men can never stand up to the sheer volume of words that gush out of a woman's mouth. Nor can women endure the brute strength their father, husband or sons have. Men and women also heal from emotional and relational wounds differently.

Men have an innate need for respect and are visually oriented. They think about sex far more than you realize. By nature, men tend to be competitive. They have a driven personality and delight in adrenaline rushes. Women are more emotional, social and relationally oriented. They are constantly changing; need regular affirmations to feel loved and cared for. Women listen with their hearts and think with their feelings. Women have greater need to connect with their mate and look forward to spending time together sharing about life issues. Especially when she is stressed or hurt or confused, she wants to share with her mate to release the burdens of life.

Change: Tweaking Each Other
In our first year of marriage, we made several unsuccessful attempts at "hammering and chiseling" at each other to reshape the other

into our mental image of a spouse. Having married late, we were very set in our ways and resisted any change from the other. We felt frustrated that we weren't making much headway and gave it up (though not completely!).

Many women marry men hoping to change them. Men marry women hoping that they would be accepted as they are and they will not be nagged. Similarly, men come into marriage trying to carve their bride into a work of art—the dream girl of his imagination, while she is hoping against hope that her "prince charming" will not discover her flaws! In marriage, the bride and groom often end up in a tug-of war where they are trying to change the other person into their mental image.

Instead of trying to mold our spouses into our ideal, we can learn about and appreciate our partners for who they are. It is hard to accept our partners if we do not feel secure about ourselves, because differences symbolize separation and

What counts in making a happy marriage is not so much how compatible you are, but how you deal with incompatibility.
– Leo Tolstoy

incompatibility to many people. The more insecure people are, the more they feel threatened by differences, and the harder it is to be close to a partner who is dissimilar. A secure woman can love the fact that her husband enjoys reading international politics, even though she can never make any sense of it.

By nature, I (Sam) tend to be visionary. I see the big picture quickly, I try to stay ahead of the world by keeping track of emerging issues and trends, and come from a corporate business background. I see the world from thirty thousand feet in the sky. On the contrary, Mary is a pharmaceutical research scientist, who gives importance to the minutest details (even at the molecular level!), giving utmost attention to the nitty-gritty details of everything. I am more like a telescope and Mary is like a microscope. We both look at the same things so differently!

Mary tries to make me see things that do not appear on my radar and I find it to be so frustrating to paint the bigger picture. Though we see such distinct perspectives, we should not lose our uniqueness and become like the other. A "bi-focal" spectacle is the best metaphor for our marriage—possessing both microscopic and telescopic vision for our life, marriage and calling. It keeps us from being myopic believing that my way of doing things as the only way or thinking my way is the right way.

Designer: Purpose Behind Differences

Our Creator designed the sexes with a purpose. Our distinctions are made for a greater purpose and not to prove superiority of one over the other. The divine blueprint of marriage between one man and one woman, for a lifetime, is remarkable. The original design for marriage intends for us to be different. Marriage is not meant to be between

"But at the beginning of creation God 'made them male and female'. For this reason a man will leave his father and mother, be united to his wife and two will become one flesh. So they are no longer two, but one. Therefore what God has joined together, let man not separate."
– Mark 10:6–9

people of the same sex. We are fashioned to complement each other and perfectly dovetail into each other. What an incredible design!

Rather than saying men and women are all the same or trying to turn men into women or vice versa, why don't we take a step back, acknowledge the intrinsic differences and thank God for them. Acknowledge the Creator's ingenuity and make the differences deepen our relationship according to God's manual for marriage. The divine order is for a husband to love his wife and a wife to respect her husband. One of the fundamental needs wired into a man's soul is the need for respect and that of a woman is the need for love.

We believe in the divine design of marriage as a man–woman covenant for life. The creation story tells us after creating the world, God sets to create humankind in his own image. God created us distinctively as man and woman. The order of marriage requires man to leave his parents and to be united with his wife and the two to become one. The mystery of marriage is that two distinct persons, without losing their individuality and personhood, become one. This process does not happen overnight with the wedding ceremony or sexual union, but requires a lifelong journey as husband and wife. We are constantly in the process of becoming, being transformed into greater unity and growing oneness through the differences, struggles, and challenges along the way.

It is important to note that God commands the man to leave his parents, contrary to many cultures where women have to leave her parents and join her husband's ancestral home. The biblical model gives priority to the new relationship over every relational bond, for that is the only way to build a strong union. As long as parents are involved or driving our lives, we will fail to create mutuality in the newly forged marriage. Without leaving parents, cleaving does not happen, and without proper cleaving, couples do not become one flesh. Of course, it does not mean that just because we got married, we abandon or dishonor our parents and fail to carry out our duties toward our parents as they age.

Making Differences Work: Complement

Neither of you are right or wrong in any particular view of your differences. One is not better than the other, it is simply different. Making those differences work toward strengthening your relationship requires empathetic understanding and thoughtful action, instead of allowing differences to drive a wedge between you both. In fact, the difference hold an amazing possibility to deepen your appreciation for each other's uniqueness and strengthen your marriage.

The first step to making differences work for you, is understanding your mate or fiancé(e). Part of the problem is that both men and women think he/she understands the other. But the fact is that you don't understand your mate nearly as well as you think you do. Before marriage, you and your partner were trying to woo each other and present your best behaviors. You even gloss over glaring differences in each other, but after the wedding even small irritants are a big deal and can cause serious rifts in the relationship.

Take a hard look at your differences before you marry, including your view of genders and your own specific attitudes, thoughts and expectations. Resist the temptation to overlook some differences that come up or the tendency to think your love is strong enough to overlook some major differences. Some people with poor self-esteem or who are very self-centered expect to find a mates who will make them happy. They may dream of mates who are beautiful, wealthy or who can magically intuit their every want and take away every hurt they have ever felt.

What counts in making a harmonious marriage is not how similar you are, but how you handle your differences.

Such people need to work on themselves; seek professional help, because finding mates will rarely make them feel better until they are first happy with themselves. They have to leave the childish role of expecting life to provide for them with a lifelong caretaker and start giving themselves to others.

When a wife does what makes her husband happy, she is happy. Also, when he does what makes her happy, he will be happy. They can agree to disagree about politics and other issues on which they do not agree. You both maybe as different as night and day. He is a morning person, she is a night owl. He is very organized, she is terribly disorganized. He loves routine, she is impulsive. He is meticulous, she is easy going. You may like different foods, listen to different music and play different games. As much as these differences can lead to arguments and conflict, they also hold possibilities of interesting conversations as you learn from each other and share opposing points of view. You need not have to renounce your views and accept your mate's view as your own in order to be happily married.

An insecure woman feels threatened by differences because she wants to share everything with her husband. She will try to pull him away from the television and want to talk about her day at home or work. She feels inadequate when others appreciate a part of him that she cannot. She also worries that he will stop loving her if he meets women who discuss issues with him that she does not understand or appreciate. For women, flowers and chocolate are more important than for men. When she feels loved and appreciated, she is more confident, sexually responsive and fulfilled in life.

Likewise, some men enjoy a wife's career success because it relieves their economic burden. They are glad when their wife finds work fulfilling, for this makes the women happier and more interesting to be around. Insecure men are afraid of women who have fulfilling careers, fearing that, if they get married, the wife might stop needing him, or might meet men who could become the husbands' rivals. Some men deliberately seek wives who are limited and insular in order to get more attention than their wives do; their wives will always look up to them. In cases where wives are more educated and make more money than husbands, conflicts can arise out of faulty thinking of power sharing and misunderstanding of roles.

One of the opportunities marriage offers is learning how to complement our way of perceiving and understanding. A large part of why we feel marriage is essential is because it provides an awesome opportunity to mature in our thinking and enrich the meaning of life. We come to a deeper understanding of otherness and what togetherness can accomplish. We learn to know and serve each other well. Marriage causes us to really grow up!

Exercise 5: Gender Quotient

1. What was your earliest awareness of your gender?

2. What was your earliest awareness of the opposite gender?

3. How differently did you relate to same-gender siblings and opposite-gender siblings?

4. Describe how you felt being attracted to someone of the opposite sex for the first time.

5. How did your mom and dad divide their roles?
   Bread-winner/Homemaker

   Who made decisions in your home?

   Who handled finances at home?

   Who led in matters of faith?

6. What gender stereotypes are commonly held by your friends? Why?

- Women working outside of home

- Women should take care of children

- Father will discipline

- Women should cook and clean the house

- Shopping

- Managing the finances

- Man is the head of the family

- Boys are preferred over girls

- Others _____

- _____

Past Matters
Taking Off Our Masks

A good marriage is between two good forgivers. (Ruth Bell Graham)

By his wounds, we are healed. (Isaiah 53:5)

Sara, a tall, attractive, computer programmer lamented as she talked about her recent breakup with Sunil, whom she had known for over two years. "It is so hard. I'm so depressed. Why did he dump me? I don't get it. We were going steady and even talked about marriage," she kept sobbing.

Then she continued, "I never saw this coming. Is there anything wrong with me? He'll never find anyone who will be as good to him as I was. Why was I abandoned? Why can't I find a decent guy?" Sara's tearful lament was nothing new to her. This was not the first time a guy had deserted her. She had a history of relationships with men since her college days and a series of breakups. Many men took advantage of her giving and caring nature, used and abused her for their own selfish needs and eventually left her for other women.

Working through our past hurts and pains are an important

preparation for marriage that every single must take up seriously. Past relationships, childhood abuse, dysfunctional homes that you had grown up in, sexual experimentations etc. have a tremendously negative impact on your marriage. If we are not honest with our past or fail to deal with it conclusively, it can sabotage intimacy and growth in your marriage.

Past emotional, relational and sexual blunders can cast a long shadow into your marriage. No one is perfect and everyone brings some form of baggage as they tie the knot. The ghosts of your mate's childhood abuse can haunt you for rest of your married life. Whether you are a survivor or the mate of a survivor, healing from the past is vital to building relational intimacy.

Masked Marriages: Hiding Behind

When they walk down the wedding aisle to tie the knot, most people are oblivious of how their past could impair their future hopes. We try many half-hearted approaches in dealing with our past. We live in denial or consciously try to forget it and put it behind. We may be unaware of weights that we are dragging into our marriage. We may minimize them or rationalize them. Our focus on future hopes can keep us blinded to unresolved issues of the past and how they can obliterate our marriage.

Many couples enter into marriage with masks. Newlyweds cover up some aspect of their life before their mate, sometimes out of shame or because they do not want to weigh down the other person with their problems. But the tragic aspect of such relationships is that even after marriage they continue to play the same game, hiding things from each other.

Masks are worn to conceal the past ranging from casual lies to serious personal wounds, childhood neglect to verbal abuse, infatuation to sexual activity, broken relationship to abortion, and substance addiction to the death of a close friend or relative. Some of these hurts are inflicted because of willful personal choice and some out of ignorance. Others out of rebellion or experimentation. Often, we are unaware of the consequences of our decisions or shameful actions. Some masks are to cover up what others have done to you. Whatever the case maybe, we try to cover up the scars from past hurts and failures with superficial make-up. We tend to think that time will heal and reduce the effects of shame or assume that it will hurt less in the future. We try to forget about it and want to move on with life.

Some are getting married to the masks, not the real person behind the mask, and the rest of the marriage becomes disillusioned in their search for true self. They sense they married the wrong person or have been cheated. Masked people live in perpetual fear of exposure or with the nagging question— "What if my spouse finds out who I really am?"

> *Bear with each another and forgive whatever grievances you may have against one another. Forgive as the Lord forgave you.*
> *– Paul (Colossians 3:13)*

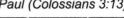

This is called the "Jacob predicament" after the story of the Jewish patriarch. He was in love with Rachel, but was tricked to marry her less attractive sister. He had worked seven years as the bride price to earn Rachel, but on the wedding night he was deceived by her father to marry Leah instead. The father-in-law yield to the custom of the day to get the older one married first, and at the same time agrees to give the younger daughter Rachel if Jacob works for another seven years. Jacob felt cheated and given an unfair deal by being forced to marry Leah. He had to deal with jealousy and rivalry between his wives and the generational curse continued down to future generations. Imagine the plight of a guy who was living and working for his father-in-law, seeing his sweetheart probably every day, but was forcefully married to her sister.

Masked marriages cause being in love with one, but being married to another. We all tend to portray an image about ourselves that is better than our real self. We lack the courage to bare our souls to someone else. We do not want others to know about our past failures or the dark side of our lives. We fear that we might fall in their sight or they will not appreciate our candor.

Modern marriages exhibit a dichotomy between an image and reality. A portrayal of our true identity often differs from the reality. This is particularly true in cultures where parents boast about their children and paint an idealistic picture in order to get them married. Thereafter, the couple tries to live up to that portrayed image and fails to come to terms with some of the hard realities about themselves.

Often, one mask forces you to put on other masks. Hiding things only leads to hiding more things. Cover ups only pile up over time. We block out memories that are too painful to bear in the juggling between several masks and constantly trying to live up to the bloated expectation of the other and the world around us, we lose ourselves. I do not know who I am? There is no place that I can simply be me!

In some African cultures, parents give the "mask of a stunning beauty" to the bride wishing her a good marriage. Homes of young couples are adorned with the mask. The truth is far from it. Only marriages without any mask are stable and grow stronger over time. Entering into an intimate relationship with masks is extremely dangerous.

Transparency is key to building strong relational bonds. Being able to speak your mind and having nothing to hide establishes a climate of deep trust and mutual respect. When both partners are confident that their mutual acceptance is not contingent on their performance and there is room for failure, it creates an environment where people can be real with each other. We all are fallible and need to learn to forgive each other which is a linchpin of a strong marriage.

Mate's Baggage: Embrace

As if personal baggage was not enough, in marriage your mate's baggage gets dumped in your lap too. Even as you are thinking about your future blissfulness of married life, the past replays before you, and to be honest some of it can be haunting. The same is going through your mate's mind as well. Stop being oblivious to hard realities and prepare to acknowledge your mate's baggage as well.

Whether you discover them accidently or your mate admits them to you, it can be very traumatic. It is hard to accept unpleasant past and present behaviors that you had never seen until date. It is not easy to stumble upon the fact that your fiancé(e) had previous relationship or lost virginity or your new husband is addicted to pornography. It sets in disillusionment and confusion. It will generate lots of questions in your mind and some strong feelings. It would make you doubt your decision to be with that person for the rest of your life. The more severe the baggage, the more intense the feelings it will

> *The injured party does not want to be compensated because he has been wronged; he wants to be healed because he has been hurt.*
> – G.K. Chesterton

bring about. You would wonder why the person kept you in the dark and why he/she chose to reveal it now. When exposed, it is natural to feel cheated and deception can significantly undermine your relationship.

The start of the marriage is a poor time for such disclosure and can create resentment and aversion. It is always better to clean up a soiled past before the marriage and prepare to walk down the aisle clean. If needed, seek professional help in dealing through difficult pasts. Agonizing memories of incest or child molestation or unwanted pregnancies would require the help of a professional in sorting things out.

When it comes to baggage in marriage, admission is better than discovery. Maybe you never shared some things from your past with anyone before and do not know how to articulate them, but you must come clean about your past with your marriage partner for it lays a strong foundation of honesty and transparency in your relationship. One can prepare one's mate before blurting out the soiled past. Recognize how such admission can hurt the other and seek his/her help in moving beyond it. Together, a couple can deal with the past and move toward wholeness. They can hold each other accountable and a loving, trusting and a forgiving partner can be a powerful agent in healing the past and bonding one's relationship.

If not told about some of your mate's past, be assured after marriage you are bound to discover some not so pleasant things about your mate; not great and exciting aspects, but also the disturbing and scary side. Everyone has some form of dark side. Are you willing to be graceful and extend some unconditional acceptance, no matter what your mate's past be? Accepting your mate's past marks the beginning of a great marriage. Threatening pasts, circumstances, and behaviors are not sidestepped; instead, they are seen as opportunities to learn something about your partner and building a strong relationship.

Digging Deeper: Dealing with Our Past

Dealing with one's past can be a frightening experience. No one likes to exhume one's past hurts or relive painful moments all over again. Revisiting soul wounds can be a draining experience and our natural response is to cover it up and make things look normal, yet it is the best thing to do in building a strong marital bond.

Our common reaction to unpleasant life experiences, whether it is something we chose to do or something that has been done to us, is to ignore it or try to forget about it. We try to put it behind us and keep moving on. But some of the wounds have become so much a part of who we are that there is no escape from them.

They tend to come along with us wherever we go. We shove them under the rug, not knowing that it keeps rotting under there and the stench gets worse by the day. There are skeletons in a closet that no one else knows about and gets opened wide in your face after the wedding. Many couples walk down the wedding aisle with finest clothes and broadest smiles, yet unaware of how some of their past is going to explode like a volcano with molten lava burning up joy and intimacy in the marriage.

Some brush it aside as an insignificant incidence and do not know how it can haunt future relationships. Many of us resist looking at past hurts and hope to keep them buried. Still others think they have dealt with the past long ago and had forgiven their offenders. Even if we have finished with the pain, the pain

Our achievements of today are but the sum total of our thoughts of yesterday. You are today where the thoughts of yesterday have brought you and you will be tomorrow where the thoughts of today take you.
– Blaise Pascal

has not finished with us yet. Repressed childhood pain can burst within an intimate relationship, like marriage.

Many have pain from growing up in dysfunctional homes. People most often repeat relational patterns they are familiar with or exposed. Prolonged exposure to certain behavior patterns of your parents, how they talked or resolved issues becomes the guide in relating to your mate after you get married. In most cases, pain of a broken home is not dealt with, it gets repeated. The vast majority of our feelings, sensations, attitudes and reactions are acted out in relationships with our conscious awareness. Our subconscious self is like the large submerged part of the iceberg, and if we are not aware, our future spouse and marriage can collide with the hidden past and be shipwrecked.

Pain is God's megaphone. Pain is only a symptomatic feeling that something is fundamentally wrong with us. Without pain, we would not know that there was a problem and an infection could grow. Pain creeps into the dark recesses of our mind and continues to contaminate our relational health and capacity. Our inability to deal with pain is a much bigger problem than the pain itself.

A band-aid is a poor solution to deep-seated psychological pain from the past. A pseudo-cure or half-hearted approach to seeking healing are also dangerous when it comes to serious issues like emotional or physical abuse, rape, persistent addiction, divorce or death of a parent. It must be dealt with decisively and permanently. We must diffuse this tension and incapacitate its power to ruin your present and future.

Do not surprise your mate by launching into past hurts unexpectedly. Prepare your mate. Find the right time and place to bring out the past. Deal with one issue at a time. Be truthful and sincere. Take personal responsibility. Seek forgiveness and help in overcoming failures and hurts. Hold the relationship more dear than the issues.

Baggage Claim: Handling Hurts, Habits & Hang-ups

A few months ago, I was waiting in line to check in for a flight at a large American airport. The airline industry had been struggling in recent years and had cut many of its regular services. Unaware of the changes in baggage policy, I tried to check in a bag, and they told me I had to pay for it. Then the attendant went on to make a statement that stuck with me for a while. She said, "You've got to pay for your baggage!"

That is true of life. We all carry some kind of baggage. Baggage are wounds from our past that still hurt and continue to undermine our relational and emotional health. It can arise from parental neglect, which manifest as a lack of love and attention from parents or parents who could spend lots of money but never had any time to give to their children. Or, it can be due to something that has been done to you like inappropriate touching or molestation by a cousin or uncle. It could be more serious things like emotional blackmail, sexual abuse or rape. But you know the kind of things that we keep stuffed deep below that still hurts. You try to cover up these hurts with lipstick and plastic smiles, but they never go away.

Dealing with baggage may vary from person to person and experience to experience. Some carry it on shoulders, while others carry in their hands. Some temporarily check it in at one place, only to collect it little later at another place. We roll it on wheels and make it easier to carry it around. Nevertheless, the heaviness is too much, and the burdens tend to take its toll over a period of time, especially in relationships.

In the pursuit of happily-ever-after, it is absolutely essential to heal and recover from emotional baggage. If you would not carry large suitcases when you walk down the aisle on the biggest day of your life, why would you want emotional baggage to lie hidden beneath your marriage? It is better to come clean with past before the wedding than to let it blow up in your face afterwards.

There is a concept of warped mirror in relationships. It simply means failing to recognize our own failures, which leads to expecting much more in our mate than we would demand even of ourselves. It takes work to look deep into our own heart to see how we could be a better spouse and what we have to offer to our mate rather than mandating what others should offer to us. Baggage is like the huge iron ball chained to your feet. An athlete could never think of making it to the finish line no matter how hard he tries, it keeps holding him back and dragging backwards. Weight on your feet will hinder your pace and keep you from making any progress. Past baggage often comes between a couple and can wreck their marriage. Learn the art of baggage handling before you walk down the aisle. The lesser the baggage and the better handling of baggage before a couple ties the knot, the better their prospects are of a stronger marriage.

Climate of Forgiveness: Pulling Off the Masks

Whether you are a survivor of past blunders or the mate of a survivor, healing from the past is crucial to building relational intimacy. Begin your relationship on a clean slate, as much as possible. The test of your love and commitment to each other will depend on how well you deal with the dirty linens of the past and present. Taking-off your mask also holds the potential to deepen your trust and intimacy. A climate of total transparency helps any relationship to flourish and grow.

"Forgive and forget. Move on. It will be okay." These are well-worn clichés, which are easier to say than to practice. Forgiveness is never easy, yet very essential in building strong marriages. The past will always be there with us, for we cannot erase it from our lives. But what we can do is to destroy its power in affecting our lives, relationship and future.

Forgiveness is renouncing your right to get even with your mate for the agony they have inflicted on you, whether through direct retaliation or just letting bitterness fester. Let your forgiveness be unconditional, willing and repeated. Learn and practice the concept of "advance forgiveness"—resolving and expressing that future hurts of your mate will also be forgiven. It does not enable you to continue in bad behavior, but awakens a desire to please your mate and never to go down that route again. Do for others what you would like them to do for you.

Allow each other to make mistakes; let go of resentment and hurt. Let your mate know that he/she does not have to be a perfect person in the marriage. They can be real and transparent in every thought, word and deed. Cut each other slack as you work through tough areas and focus on positive solutions. Practice grace, which is a combination of unconditional acceptance and forgiveness and watch how your marriage grows.

Wounded Healers: Walking in Wholeness

We all carry scars from our past. Some wounds leave behind permanent scars even when fully healed, while others grow fresh skin over the wounds, leaving no signs of damage whatsoever. When we recognize our past baggage, it is easier to forgive the past of our mate's. This mutual recognition and forgiveness bring emotional and relational health to the marriage.

We become healing agents to each other in marriage. You must not allow memories and past wounds to spill into the lives of those you love and your future together. Your home becomes a place of healing and freedom to pursue authentic relationships and build healthy emotional intimacy with your mate. Thus, marriage brings healing and wholeness to life, leading to deeper meaning and purpose of living.

Exercise 6a: Baggage Claim

You must come clean with your past, personal, relational and sexual baggage. Our past choices can affect our marriage relationship. Instead of covering up our past, this exercise will help you to become transparent before your mate and win their trust. All of us have some skeletons in our closet. Digging up our buried secrets can be difficult and painful, yet it is very important not to keep secrets in an intimate relationship like marriage.

You should prayerfully prepare yourself. You need to gather courage, articulate, and prepare to experience pain again as you revisit your past and seek understanding and forgiveness from your mate. Anticipate disappointment and pain your mate will experience as a result of your disclosure.

Sit across a chair in a private place. Imagine your mate is sitting across from you on the chair and rehearse how you will describe your past.

As your mate shares about his/her past baggage, be prepared to forgive and not hold it against him/her ever in the future. Appreciate your mate's candor and assure him/her of your love.

If you think you are unable to do it because of fear of rejection or estrangement in the relationship then seek the help of a friend, counselor, pastor or relationship mentor who can help you come clean with the past.

1. Did you experience any form of abuse [physical/verbal/emotional/sexual] during your growing up years?

2. How did other emotionally and physically intimate relationships begin, was carried on and ended for you?

3. How would you prepare your mate to hear what you are going to share from your past?

4. When your mate discloses his/her past, how will you feel?

5. How will you forgive your mate when he/she shares of his/her past brokenness?

Exercise 6b: Life Map

Chronologically analyze different stages of your life, and locate major milestones in your life. Plot the milestones in the following continuum highlighting them as callouts, and develop an autobiographical sketch of your life. Please try to include any family relocation, tragedy, death, first day at school/college, religious experiences, and other emotionally significant events.

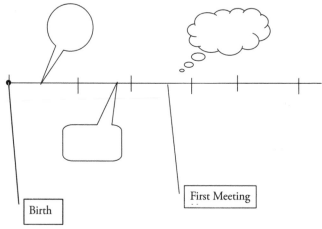

First Meeting

Birth

Date	Milestone Event	Description

Family Matters
Exploring Where You Came From

Happy families are all alike; every unhappy family is unhappy in its own way.
— From Anna Karenina *by Leo Tolstoy*

"Yet he does not leave the guilty unpunished; he punishes the children and their children for the sin of the fathers to third and fourth generation."
(Exodus 34:6, 7)

After John and Julie got married, they lived next door to John's parents, who interfered with their marriage almost every day. Julie had a difficult time relating to her mother-in-law. She felt John's mother was very demanding and did not care for her. She was expected to cook everyday and take care of his parents as well, after a busy day at work. The parents also put pressure on them to have children right away. The unkind words, conflicts and the resulting stress created lots of bitterness in their early marriage.

Taking a closer look, we find that John timidly is caught between two strong women. His mother was treating her daughter-in-law the same way she was treated by her mother-in-law when she came into that family. Men in the family were generally passive and docile, while women were in charge of the affairs of the home. John never knew how to deal with issues, as it was never modeled to him and assumed problems will be resolved over time.

We are all products of our families. Our families of origin had an indelible imprint on our consciousness, beliefs, character, lives and relationships. Whether we came from exceptional families or dysfunctional family systems, our childhood home and relationship with parents and siblings have been permanently etched in our minds and will be one of the most important influences on our marriage. This is particularly more relevant in family-oriented Asian societies than the individualistic Western society. The opinions of parents, siblings, extended families members, and even close friends weigh in when making decisions about marriage. Our parents' marriage remains forever the first marriage we see and forms our primary idea of the institution of marriage. Our understanding of roles,

> *Marriage is more about the process of learning to dance rather than finding the right dancer.*

responsibility, gender identity, cooking style etc are undoubtedly conceived in our minds from our childhood homes.

Not everything about our family of origin leaves a positive imprint. Some have grown up in less than normal family backgrounds. Fathers who are alcoholic or abusive and mothers who are neglectful or suffer from prolonged illness, significantly tarnish our concepts of family. Extended family, grandparents and even distant cousins can have a lasting influence on your future marriage.

Family Album: Know Thy Family

We might think, we know everything about our family. Maybe you come from a family that freely talks about every aspect of home life. Or maybe you come from homes where conversations were rare. Whatever the case maybe, unless we objectively reflect on our family of origin, we might not know what our mate might see in our family of origin.

So learn all you can about your own family of origin. Record pictorially your relationship with members of your family. Map at least two generations before you, like your grandparents on both sides and all siblings of your parents. Interview your parents and learn about your family before your arrival into the world or what happened when you were very small. Interview other family members close to you. Meet with your grandparents if they are still alive.

Ask yourself questions like—Is your family of origin happy? Were there any conflicts? What you wished were different at home? What fears do you have about your fiancé(e) becoming a part of your family? Try to analyze issues like how parents communicated, resolved differences, handled finances, treated children, relationship with their parents and siblings, roles, and faith issues. If parents have health challenges, discuss how you are going to take care of them in their old age.

Identify both positive and negative traits of each of your parents and each of your siblings. Honestly share your perceptions and experiences about each of them. Particularly mention how close or distant your relationship has been with each of them and why. Do not be protective or try to portray an idealistic image. If you grew up in a dysfunctional family, it may be harder to come to terms with its negative impact on you. Harder still is to share them with someone you love. Do not think what the other person is going to think about you or how they are going to accept your family members. Gather up courage to tell about your family secrets to your future mate can be extremely challenging to some. Yet it is the right thing to do. Do not leave any surprises for your mate.

If you had grown up with domestic violence or were abused by family members, it may be hard to expose it or talk about it with your mate. If you were a victim of circumstances that you had no control over or were powerless to deal with, please ensure you heal and recover from the past baggage before entering into a marriage relationship. (Make sure you have completed the exercises in previous chapter, "Past Matters: Taking Off Our Masks").

According to some family experts, one must discover one's in-laws for oneself and establish a relationship without the bias of one's mate. They say you need not dump all family dirty linen before your mate. Let him or her figure it out for him/herself. Though this independent discovery provides neutrality at the beginning of your relationship with your in-laws, it will keep you and your mate at different places when you relate to each other's families, which are not necessarily a good idea and will begin to affect your own marriage. You both must be on the same page and have a common collective stand on all matters dealing with each other's parents. You both should also be on the same page when it comes to how you deal with your own parents.

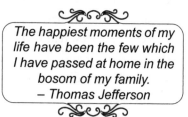

The happiest moments of my life have been the few which I have passed at home in the bosom of my family.
– Thomas Jefferson

Not Out-laws: Getting to Know Your In-Laws

Introduce your side of the family person by person to your fiancé(e) and get to know each other's family through the eyes of your mate. As you mutually learn about each other's families, refuse to condemn or create negative feeling towards each other's parents. None of us have perfect parents; neither will you be a perfect couple. Graciously accept your in-laws and honor them as you would honor your own parents.

As you describe your own family of origin to your mate, begin with positive traits. Before you begin exposing the dark side of your family, prepare your mate to hear some hard realities that your mate is getting into. Extend grace to each other as your get to know each other. Do not form opinions about in-laws based on your mate's past experiences, but develop feelings based on your own interactions. Learn more about particularly your mate's opposite-gender parent. Your mate's expectations of you are often formed from the opposite gender parent. For example, a new groom would expect his bride to cook like his mother and a new bride would expect her man to do chores around the house like her father. Understanding your in-laws for who they are will help you understand why your mate acts or thinks the way they do. Remember the first and most influential marriage that we have is that of our parent's.

Early on in our marriage, I (Sam) realized that Mary's Dad had a significant place in her life. She adored her father and many of her attitudes and demeanors can be traced back to him. So I took it upon myself to study my father-in-law. When I visited him by myself, I took time to hang around with him. I drove him to places and spent extended periods of time along with him, often asking several questions about family life. I enquired about

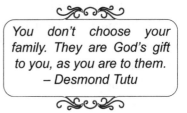

> You don't choose your family. They are God's gift to you, as you are to them.
> – Desmond Tutu

his side of the family, his career, raising family, challenges faced, and belief system and even debated on some of his favorite topics. All of which was intended at getting to know him and the influence he had on my wife!

When both of you are aware of issues your respective families have and are careful to draw clear boundaries not letting them affect your relationship and it will help you deal with them as a team. Talking candidly about your family problems will help not carry forward those negative traits. When we fail to name these traits and destroy its power, it is most likely to creep into your own home without your knowledge.

Neither your parents nor your future in-laws are a perfect people. Ignore their drawbacks and do not hold grudges against them. Break the cycle of destructive habits and generational sins. Give a fresh start to your family life and start afresh some new God-honoring family traditions. If you do not do anything, they will get passed on into your marriage. Generational sins causes bondage affecting the quality of life and marriage, and it might even continue on to future generations.

Take the best from both sides of the family. You must objectively analyze and identify traits that you want to emulate in your family and what negative ones you would like to put an end to. Together you must decide to eliminate some of the inherited and harmful patterns from the past and hold each other accountable to the new standards you have set for your own family life.

It is recommended that you live separately from either of your parents after the wedding, if possible. Having a home of your own will help you mark clear boundaries and establish priority of the new family unit. It will also break the reliance on your parents and make you lean on each other. It keeps parents from making decisions for you or siding with your parents. By setting up a home together, you learn a great deal about yourself and your mate, which you might not be able to if you simply move in with either of your parents. Moreover this is a clear biblical mandate to men from the first marriage. God instructs man, "to leave his father and mother. . . ."

Refrain from sharing everything about you and your mate with your parents, especially negative information. Also avoid seeking their advice on your arguments and conflicts. Their input may only further aggravate the matter. Do seek their input on issues, but do not let them do the backseat driving. If you find them intrusive into your personal affairs, you both must discuss the matter at length and arrive at a concerted stance before taking it up to your parents. For example, decisions like having a baby or buying a home should be made by the couple and not by parents or in-laws.

Genogram: Drawing Family Tree

Genogram is a technical term for a family tree diagram. It is a practical and useful way to understanding family relationships and patterns. It is a schematic plan that describes your extended family and various interpersonal dynamics. Genograms are widely used by family therapists as a tool to map family relations, giving both the therapists and the clients an overview of family relationships and patterns. Our interest is in mapping how the family we have grown up in and the many relationships we are surrounded by have impacted our very self and what we bring to our marriage.

Family trees are as old as human civilizations itself. People have kept track of their ancestries to ascertain racial or cultural purity, hoard wealth and maintain social status. In some circles pedigree was an important criteria for seeking alliance, as marriages were confined within caste and religious groups. Genograms capture family history and hierarchy by noting births, deaths, losses, connections and structures. It is widely used by family physicians, therapist and counselors.

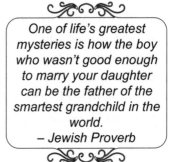

One of life's greatest mysteries is how the boy who wasn't good enough to marry your daughter can be the father of the smartest grandchild in the world.
– Jewish Proverb

The family systems theory suggests that individuals cannot be understood in isolation from one another but rather as a part of their family, as the family is an emotional unit. Families are systems of interconnected and interdependent individuals, none of whom can be understood in isolation from the system. Unlike conventional psychological theory which focuses on the individual, family systems theory encourages people to think of issues (e.g. conflict, difficult relationships, loneliness, etc.) in terms of a multigenerational family or a "system." This approach encourages people to move away from blaming others and towards individual responsibility.

Just before we got married, someone advised us to do the

genogram exercise and we greatly benefited from the analysis and have since advocated it to many couples. Each of us discovered unique things about ourselves and our family of origin which we had never known before. We drew out a detailed genogram of our respective side of the family to three generations before us. I met with our family historian and looked through several pages on my forefathers.

There are complex interplays within a family unit which can only be understood through the use of a genogram. A genogram will not only show you the names of people who belong to your family lineage, but how these relatives relate to each other. For example, a genogram will not only tell you that your Uncle George and his wife Anita have two children, but that his youngest child was sent to boarding school, that uncle George suffered from depression, was an alcoholic and a philosopher, while aunt has not spoken to her brother for years, has breast cancer and is emotionally unstable. Thus, the genograms reveals intergenerational patterns of relationship, interactions and dysfunctionalities.

> A fruit does not fall far from the tree.
> – Indian Proverb

Draw your side of the family using standard symbols recommended in the exercise page to denote individual and kinds of relationships on your family tree. Begin with your parents and siblings, and try to objectively find out more about your own family of origin. Trace back at least three generations, including both living and dead. Some amount of research may be required to find out full names, actual dates, and nature of relationship. Browse through the annals of your family history, if you have one, and interview the oldest living member on each side of the family. Look through family albums and gather pictures of people in your family tree. Software could also be used to draw out detailed genograms. Search online tools that might help you develop your family tree.

Shaking the Family Tree: Analyzing Genograms

After you have drawn your respective family trees, sit down to introduce your family schematically to each other. Merge both of your family trees by marking your relationship and date of marriage. Look for similarities and differences between both sides of the families. Find out distinctive features of each generation or family units. What were they best known for or what they were notorious for? Look for repeated patterns and inherited traits. Birth order characteristics and gender roles can be compared. Closely track ethnicity, race, migration, socio-economic class, education and profession across generations. Also identify chronic illness, accidents, deaths, divorces, age of marriage, number of children etc.

Soon after our wedding, when we were doing our rounds to visit relatives we would carry our genogram and say "we are going to see this uncle or that grandma" and both of us knew exactly who we were talking about. One of the characteristics that we mapped was age of marriage as we both had waited much more than our peers. At our singles and premarital seminars I often get asked when one should get married.

So what is the right age to get married? In every community and culture there seems to be an unspoken assumption concerning the age by which they would like to see everyone married. Parents begin to put pressure on children at a much earlier age have proven that getting married early or late is harmful for the health of the marriage. Child marriages might have happened in traditional societies a few generations ago, but are less likely to survive today. Lack of maturity, relational skills and financial resources can undermine such a marriage greatly. Getting married later in life after prolonged singlehood is also not helpful in building a healthy marriage. Difficult adjustments, ticking biological clock and emotional baggage cause strain in the marriage.

Not so long ago, a young couple, Jackie and Jenny, came to see us for premarital counseling. As the lovers walked in they seemed to be joined together at their hip and were gazing into each other's eyes. They sat down on the couch so close we thought one might end up on other's lap!

Jackie began, "Thanks for seeing us. We just announced our engagement, but our parents think we're too young to get married." Jenny nodded as she looked adoringly into his eyes. They squeezed each other's hands tightly.

"Well, how old are you?" I asked.

"I'm nineteen," he said, "and Jenny will be eighteen in few months."

"But why does age matter anyway?" Jenny tagged on. "We love each other and we're right for each other. Everything else will work out."

I did not want to be biased against them and tried to be as open-minded as possible. Who knows, sometimes eighteen-year-olds can be surprisingly mature and committed in a relationship. As we continued our conversation, I learned he had dropped out of high school and she was trying to finish her final year of schooling. Then I asked Jackie, "How do you envision your life in ten years?"

"I love talking to people. I'm good with bikes and cars," he replied. "So, I might end up as an auto salesman or something. But I'm not really sure what I'll do for a career or where we might live or any of that. All I know is that if Jenny and I are together, we'll be fine. We can make it through anything."

"How about you, Jenny?" I inquired.

"Oh. . .I will be with Jackie wherever he takes me. I know we will be happy together," she responded.

Now I was beginning to be concerned about this relationship. It was high on fantasy and low on reality. When I further probed both about how they describe themselves, family of origin, personal strength and weaknesses, styles of communications, conflict handling etc, I received more vague answers. They fumbled for answers and repeatedly ended up with "love will see us through" statements.

Finally I said, "Thanks for coming by and sharing your life with us. We want to tell you the truth as clearly as we know how. And the truth is: all those warm fuzzy feelings are necessary in marriage, but they might evaporate when the rubber hits the road. It is more important for you to know who you are as individuals, be clear with what you want to do in life and where you are headed before making a marital commitment."

My advice did not go well with the starry-eyed lovers. But I had to tell them the truth. Over four-fifth of couples under twenty years of age end up in divorce. The reasons attributed to this high marital fatality are immaturity, confusion over marital roles, inability to earn a living, and continuing education. So, what is best age to get married? There is no fixed age bracket where everyone should be married. It depends on your personality, emotional maturity and readiness to enter into marriage. Statistically, marriage seems to be more stable when it begins no earlier than the mid twenties, although legal limits are eighteen for women and twenty-one for men.

Exercise 7a: Genogram

A genogram is symbolic representation of one's family relationships. It helps to visualize the entire family network and their interworkings. It helps you to identify relational patterns and inherited tendencies.

Draw a family tree and map out at least 3 generations (grandparents, parents, yours) and all your first cousins. Try to locate individual and relational characteristics that come to your mind when you think of them. Describe both positive and negative experiences you had with each of them. Map out any area of interest that you want to see generational patterns (Alcoholism, Drugs, Smoking, Illness, Education, Profession, Place lived, Relational, Behavior, Affective, Conflicts, Traditions etc).

Standard Symbols for Genograms

Exercise 7b: Family of Origin

Among the choices given, please select one that is closest to in your family of origin. Exchange answers with your fiancé(e). Which experience of your fiancé(e) is most different from yours? Discuss what impact this might have on your future marriage.

1. Affection was:

A. Shown warmly and often

B. Rarely shown in public

C. Other _____

2. My home was usually:

A. Neat and clean

B. Comfortably cluttered

C. Other _____

3. Decision making was done by:

A. Father

B. Mother

C. Both parents in consultation

D. Everyone in the home (including the kids)

E. Default (Nobody seemed to make decisions. Life just happened.)

4. When my parents disagreed or fought:

A. They yelled and screamed

B. One usually gave in to the other

C. They compromised

D. They separated to cool off

E. One or both used the "silent treatment"

F. I wouldn't know. They never fought in front of me.

5. Responsibility for keeping the home picked up belonged to:

A. Everyone picked up after themselves

B. Mother or father picked up after the kids

C. I never noticed. It was never an issue.

D. Nobody picked up. (It was pretty messy.)

6. Privacy was:

A. Respected

B. A sign of secretiveness and selfishness

C. _____

7. Money was:

A. Saved for a rainy day

B. Spent only on necessities

C. We were always in debt

D. Used freely for recreational pursuits

E. Other _____

8. Relationships were:

A. Close. We had many times of fun together.

B. Cordial, but each person primarily recreated by themselves

C. Strained

9. Household chores were divided according to:

A. "Women's work" or "Men's work"

B. Who had the most time or skill at the chore

C. Both parents took equal responsibility

10. On Christmas, we:

A. Put a tree up and decorated early

B. Christmas Eve was the big celebration when we opened presents

C. Santa Claus decorated the tree when the kids were asleep and we opened gifts on Christmas morning.

D. We're non-Christians and don't celebrate Christmas

E. Other _____

Communication Matters
Talking It Over

A deaf husband and a blind wife are always a happy couple. (Danish Proverb)

The right word at the right time is like a custom-made piece of jewelry.
(Proverbs 25:11 Message).

Jimmy and Julie have grew up in the same neighborhood and were casual acquaintances. After graduating in engineering, he moved to another city for a new job. In his loneliness and demanding career, he shot emails to several of his old friends and only Julie had responded and encouraged him. Julie was about to graduate from college and needed guidance on vocational choices. She found his input and advice very helpful. Soon they began calling each other and enjoyed their time together.

When her parents began to put pressure on Julie to consider a marriage proposal that had come to them, she was confused and not ready to consider marriage. That evening when Jimmy called, she shared about the marriage proposal. He also shared how his parents were putting pressure on him to get married now that he had finished school and was well employed. They were able to understand each other's predicaments and provide comfort.

The more they shared and bared their souls to each other, the more emotionally entangled they became. They began to share their fears and hopes. Both secretly desired and longed for each other, but did not know how to take the next step. Both felt they are made for each other and neither could see themselves married to anyone else. He wondered if he should express his love and propose to her or go through his parents to approach her parents. Julie was scared to tell her parents about how she feels about Jimmy. Both were shy and having no experience in relationship matters before, felt confused and uncertain about the strange feelings they have for each other. They did not know what they should do next or how to go about it.

Good communication is indispensable to any healthy relationship. It affects every aspect of marriage and is vital for growing in intimacy. We communicate content, intent, emotions, attitudes, and beliefs through verbal and non-verbal means. Lack of proper communication can hurt marriages immensely and might take lots of effort to recover from its damage. By it, we listen, express, negotiate, explain, inform, compliment and share with each other. By it we argue, quarrel, criticize, justify, put down and condemn each other. Also, without communication we give the silent treatment, withdraw and isolate each other, which are destructive to relational growth.

We live in an era with numerous technological innovations that aid communication, yet we struggle to communicate effectively within marriage. On a daily basis we are influenced by professional mass media communication and subliminal messages. We are bombarded and manipulated by slick advertisements and persuaded to new lifestyles and value systems. We are exposed to more media, yet we struggle to deeply converse one-on-one with the love of our lives. What a strange dilemma! Tools and techniques can be helpful, but if we do not acquire basic skills everything else is useless.

Art of Communication: Transparency

Good communication is more than mere exchange of information. It is the sharing of lives and intertwining of souls. It helps to know each other and to be known by each other. It can be done with one other person over a lifetime and it requires consistency and faithfulness, and results in transparency and intimacy. It is more of an art and less of a science.

Understanding each other's communication styles and establishing some positive conventions early on are important to any marriage. Undoing some inherited patterns and adopting new methods will make an enormous difference in the marital relationship. You must take time amidst your busy schedule to reconnect with each other on a regular basis and avoid potential barriers to communication between

Let your conversation be always full of grace.
– Colossians 4:6

you two. You probably know by now that it is very easy to lose trust and very hard to reclaim lost trust. You should not let your pride or ego come in the way of admitting your faults and seek apology from the other. As hard as it might sound, it is an essential skill that all fallible creatures require in an intimate relationship like that of marriage, where you cannot cover things up for long! We must intentionally and constantly work hard to get better at communicating with our mate. Both partners must work towards transparent and honest communication.

We communicate through words, tone, vocabulary, silence, gestures, touch, eyes and a variety of other ways. It involves casual conversation of daily catch up with each, letting another person know our emotions, hurts and hopes, deciding about chores, or resolving a major prolonged conflict. Effective communication deepens friendship, builds intimacy and avoids possible conflicts.

The younger generations do not make a big deal about language; it is seen only as a tool for communication and defines identity less. Every ethnic community also carries a variety of idiosyncrasies in matters of communication and gaining insight into both of your unique styles would be helpful. In the past, one partner would stay quiet in order to avoid further disagreement or escalating the conflict. But these days, couples believe in speaking their mind and consider emotional fulfillment in marriage their right. Contrary to the popular notion, disagreement helps communication. When followed through intentionally, as it open the screens of the eyes, the shutters of the mouth, the shades of the culture and the windows to the soul.

Our parents might not have said – "I love you" to each other and were reluctant to give kisses and hugs. But younger generations casually use PDA (public display of affection). Studies confirm the need for verbal affirmations of love, though our

> *The tongue has the power of life and death, and those who love it will eat its fruit.*
> *– Proverbs 18:21.*

forefathers reflected that sentiments in other ways such as providing for and protecting the family. Some people hold a negative attitude toward everything, criticizing and fault finding. Others carry ego on their shoulders or driven by customs and traditions. Some communicate indirectly (through parents or children) or with multiple meanings. Some show an ostrich-like attitude of ignoring problems, believing that if you ignore the issue, it will go away. One partner may appear to be strong and belligerent, never accepting blame, and never interested in what his/her spouse thinks. In reality, they are insecure and cover their emotional weakness by finding fault, nitpicking and carping.

Good communication is the heart of every good marriage. Learning and practicing it every day requires much work and intentionality. There is the concept of "metacommunication," which is the underlying message, the motivation behind the communication. We all need to be amateur psychologists and try to figure out what our partner really wants. For example, when Susan tells her husband that she isn't feeling well, that may be her way of saying "could you drive the children to dance lessons today, dear?" Or it may be her way of expressing a need for more attention from her spouse. We can't all be mind readers, but it is important to try to focus not just on the words being said, but what may possibly be implied as well. As with any art, communication also requires constant practice to get better and will ultimately grow your marriage closer and stronger.

Different: Style & Content

Every one of us possesses and processes communications differently. Men and women communicate very distinctively in matters of style, emotion, speed,

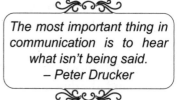

The most important thing in communication is to hear what isn't being said.
– Peter Drucker

form and content. We differ also in our thinking, language (we can speak the same language so differently!), genre, expressions, perspectives, and interpretations, making the task of really understanding what is behind the exchanges, so hard.

Generally, girls start talking earlier than boys, and then they never stop! Researchers have proven that at all stages, females talk more than males. They not only speak more often, they also speak faster (150 words per minute for women versus 120 words for men). A typical couple talks to each other ninety minutes per week , with the wife talking for sixty minutes and the husband mumbling his replies for thirty minutes. In ten years, it adds up to an excess of nearly three million more words women use than men!

Women initiate spousal conversation three times more often than men. Marriage counselors say husbands listen to only about a quarter of what their wives say and wives listen to only about half of what their husbands say. On a daily basis, women carry twice as much worry as their counterparts. No wonder they are talking so much. Men tend to talk about work, sports, politics, sex or automobiles. Women generally talk about interpersonal relationships, illness, clothes, or domestic activities, even if they work outside of home.

Women are also more emotional by nature. Men are taught not to show emotion or that it is a sign of weakness. Men sometimes feel confused by their mates' emotional outbursts and feel intimidated by them. Men and women in relationship can blackmail or manipulate each other with their emotions or lack of it.

Our upbringing and professional training also affect how we communicate. You may have grown up in a household where everyone talked about everything under the sun or interaction between family members were limited and formal in nature or somewhere in between. You might bring into your marriage same attitudes subconsciously and if your mate comes from a dissimilar background, the differing conversation styles can create unnecessary tension. Similarly, our career choices shape our vocabulary and interpersonal interaction to a great extent. If your mate is not familiar with that lingo and fails to fathom your work environment, it can create lots of misunderstanding.

Communication theory tells us that inter-personal interactions happen at five levels. First, is cliché, where you are non-sharing with the least degree of transparency. This level of interaction happens with most number of people. The second level, is factual or informational communication where you share what you know. It focuses on content over relationship. Next, is the opinion level where you share what you think. It includes your own thoughts and reflection on information. Next, is the level of emotional communication where you share what you feel. Finally, there is transparent communication where you share who you are with the highest degree of transparency. This level occurs between the least number of people. All five levels of communications will take place in a marriage and understanding them will greatly enhance your marriage relationship.

Learning to Listen: Not Just Hear

As a part of my job as a professional speaker, I (Sam) am expected to communicate to groups of people regularly. I was trained in public speaking and my corporate environment gave me ample opportunity to brush up my skills. So I thought I was good at communication. At least that is what I thought, until I got married. During courtship, we had a great time communicating with each other, though we were separated by thousands of miles. Distance made hearts grow fonder, I guess. We used all the technological inventions possible to prevent the distance coming between us. We were known to have marathon conversations (eight hours nonstop was our record)!

But early in marriage, I began to wonder why I was having a hard time in getting across to Mary. Why was she frustrated with me? Being trained as an engineer and manager, I was focused on solving problems. Every time she would bring things that happen at work or what she was thinking about, I was ready with my fixes. I would pounce on her with creative solutions to all her problems, while she simply wanted me to listen and feel understood. By constantly interrupting her and offering solution to all her problems, I only created more problems. Mr. Fix-it approach wasn't working!

Good marital communicators not only listen to the words their mates utter, but also draw meaning from those words and phrases. Listen for the feeling of the other. Men generally tend to discount the feelings of their mates. Feel how the other person feels about when they are talking. Somebody said we are given two ears but only one mouth; so listen twice as much as you speak. This is a good rule of thumb in marriage. Offering unsolicited advice or trying to "help" your mate, might prove critical.

A good listener will give focused attention to what his mate is trying to communicate and will avoid pseudo listening or selective hearing. Tuning in and out or being preoccupied with other things will not help you to focus on your mate. Focus on what is being said rather than the way it is being said, more on meaning than words. Ask questions if needed for more clarification and try to gain deeper understanding of what is being said. Resist the temptation to interrupt and jump to conclusions before your mate has finished or pass any judgments on partial information.

Rolling your eyes or yawning when your mate is trying hard to get across to you communicates your lack of interest to your mate. Try to understand the true meaning behind your spouse's words. Make an effort to understand if there's an angle or an aspect of your spouse's position that you can agree with. Flipping through newspapers or television channels or browsing the internet as you talk with your mate is a bad idea and all of which are bound to stifle good communication.

> *Be quick to listen, slow to speak.*
> *– James 1:19*

Learning to Express: Not Just Talk

Since our mates cannot read our minds, we must learn to express to our mate what on our mind and heart. In some marriages one of the mates is a non-stop talker while the other is a good listener or contemplative. Men often find it harder to articulate their thoughts and feelings compared to women. Keeping your mate in the dark or expecting the other to decipher through cryptic clues are not helpful for growing intimacy in the marriage. Psychological manipulation like stonewalling or blackmailing are dangerous to the health of any relationship.

Men are generally told not to show their feelings, it is seen as a weakness. Women tend to be expressive, yet continual nagging drives men up the wall. Open criticism involves attacking someone's personality rather than their behavior. When either or both of you get home after work, allow some "cave time" to each other, before talking about your respective days. Use phone and email to communicate with each other, but important issues must be discussed face to face.

Effective communication is a learned behavior. It is much like learning a language and requires constant practice to get better. The language of love and intimacy learning curve is steep. Like any other language acquisition, learning the love language takes effort and consistent practice. New skill development is not easy, but this one critical for your marriage. Don't expect too much too fast. They are worth the work!

Body language and non verbal signals communicate a great deal. The tone of voice, attitudes and actions speaks louder than words. Sighs, walking away, slamming doors, rolling eyes, or other gestures say a lot.

The problem with communication. . .is the illusion that it has been accomplished.
– George Bernard Shaw

Positive communication also occurs non-verbally like squeezing hands, loving embrace, sympathetic facial expression.

Honesty and truthfulness are absolutely essential in marital communication. Covering things up or witholding information to your mate are harmful attitudes, even if you think your mate is going to be upset over the information you are about to share. In fact, within a marriage you should have freedom to speak your mind and be open to sharing anything at anytime, so that you do not have to carry any burden alone. We believe within marriage, a couple should maintain total transparency and keep no secrets. Some might argue about concealing facts on professional practice and other situations. There might be some exceptions, but when it comes to anything that might affect your relationship or how you feel about the other, I believe honesty is still the best policy. Let nothing come between you two.

Communication Barriers: Speaking Different Languages

Sometime ago a married man confided to me, "My wife says I never listen to her. I think, that is what she said." Men are stereotypically said to have less communicative in relational aspects. A Jewish lady acknowledged this about men, "Our ancestors wandered in the desert for forty years because even in ancient times, men wouldn't stop to ask for directions!"

The most frequent complaint women have about their husbands is that they don't listen and the most frequent complaint men have about their wives is that they are trying to change their husbands. Men often are thinking ahead of what is being told and looking for solutions for assumed problems their wives are having. Women feel compelled to help their men improve. Men and women seldom mean the same things even when they use the same words. It seems as if both are speaking two different languages and have different needs altogether. Understanding each other's real and intended meaning requires constant translation and reinterpretation from your mate's perspective.

There are many things that come in the way of marital communication. Stress, work, children, and a constant time crunch can limit the time and energy you and your spouse have available to focus on maintaining good communication. Throw in any other factors such as aging parents, depression, illness, or financial troubles, and the challenge of maintaining healthy communication becomes even more difficult. Learn to speak your mate's language and try to meet each other's primary emotional needs, instead of giving what they needs.

There are five common communication barrier between newly married couple. First, we all carry some baggage with us from our upbringing. Our parents may have seldom communicated with each other or with us. They may have told us that children are to be seen and not heard. Second, we live in a world of television, the internet, and video games that isolate us from those nearest and dearest to us. We get comfortable finding our own meaning, purpose, and values without having to interact and communicate with others. Third, we are bombarded with outside pressure, jobs, car pools, social meetings, and the like, can steal the quality time needed for real communication between husbands and wives. Fourth, we tend to be lazy, gravitating to the nearest comfort zone. Real marital communication takes time, effort, and planning. It is not for the fainthearted. And fifth, we may be fearful of showing our emotions or of being rejected if we communicate openly and honestly.

Conflicts: Resolution

Conflicts are inevitable in all marriages. Your goal should not be to have a conflict-free marriage. Disagreements and disputes are bound to be there. It is not indicative of failure. How you handle conflict is more important than the topic of conflict. In fact, conflicts can help us develop character and personal maturity.

Argument can be destructive and undermine your relationship. Hurts over argument with your mate are more painful than same arguments with the others. It could lead to accusing, complaining, demanding, resenting, anger, holding grudges and bitterness, blaming and criticizing, all of which end up poisoning the marriage relationship. It leaves a prolonged uneasiness and you feel disconnected with your mate. We momentarily lose loving feelings of caring, trust, acceptance, understanding, appreciation and respect. Be committed to resolving conflicts at all costs. When you lose an argument and let the relationship win, you actually win. The reverse is true as well. When you win at the cost of your relationship, you actually lose.

Here are some practical tips in handling conflicts in your marriage. It is helpful to use "I messages" in conflicting situations.

"I feel angry when you are late getting home." Avoid "you messages" such as "You are always late." You have the right to feel any feeling but in conflict situations it's best to avoid "you messages" which imply judgment. It's helpful to use "proposal" language. "I propose that we only eat out once a month in order to save money." Proposal language invites the other person to negotiate with you if they don't agree with your idea. Proposal language helps couple avoid control issues. It does not exclude the other or sound unilateral.

Remember that the way you say things, your voice tone and body language, communicate more than your words. Respectful tones are helpful. In conflict resolution, avoid threats of violence; threats to end the relationship; bringing up several issues at the same time; sarcasm; absolutes ("you never" or "you always"); name calling or labeling ("you are a bully" or "that is childish"); dwelling on the past.

> *Marriage is one long conversation, checkered with disputes.*
> *– Robert L. Stevenson*

There are several red flags to watch for in relationships. See if you or your fiancé(e) is lying or truthful in all matters. Do you tend to speak white lies or trying to be nice to each other with lies? If your relationship starts and is based on deceptions, it can lead to more serious troubles later. Cover-ups only lead to more cover-ups and the lying person will try to live the lie in order to continue to impress the partner. You must have the courage to bare your soul and not hold anything back, in order for your relationship to flourish. You should also accept the person as he/she is. Extend grace to his lies and failures (we all have some) and promise to be true to each other.

It is important to be creative and look for more ways to cut back where you can and schedule more time in your marriage for communication. Ideally, you want to have some time each day when you and your spouse can touch base and share with each other. If that's not possible, then you certainly want to make it a top priority each week to find a time for relaxed, emotionally intimate conversation. Without good communication, you and your spouse are in danger of losing heart connection. As your time to listen, and share from the heart with your partner is negatively impacted by life events, it's crucial that communication blocks be kept to a minimum. You need to get the most from the limited time that you do have.

Finally remember, if you don't have a healthy way of communicating your thoughts and feelings to each other, of speaking and being heard, then everything else will ultimately crumble.

Exercise 8: Communication Styles

1. Share with each other your childhood and practice your listening skills.

2. What do you appreciate most about your mate's communication?

3. What frustrates or concerns you about your mate's communication style?

4. How easy or hard is it for you to share your inner feelings? Why?

5. Place an "X" on the continuum below that describes your level of comfort in sharing feelings. Also mark an "O" that you think best describes your mate.

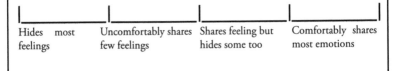

| Hides most feelings | Uncomfortably shares few feelings | Shares feeling but hides some too | Comfortably shares most emotions |

6. Which of the emotions seem easy or difficult to express for you and your mate?

Emotions	Self		Your Mate	
	Easy to Express	Difficult to Express	Easy to Express	Difficult to Express
Love				
Fear				
Anger				
Pleasure				
Anxiety				
Happiness				
Hurt				
Frustration				
Disappointment				
Shame				
Others				

7. Read the following statements and mark where you stand (put "X" for yourself and "O" for your mate).

	Usually	Sometimes	I Need Improvement
Good listener			
Empathetic			
Courteous			
Boastful			
Exaggeration			
Truthful			
Speak rudely			
Gossip			
Trustworthy			
Anger			
Forgiveness			
Talkative			
Open communication			
Direct & forceful			
Nagging			
Complaining			
Analytical			
Problem avoider			
Conflict resolver			
Others			

8. How do you want your mate to communicate love to you? How do your mate want you to communicate love to him/her?

9. What major conflicts have you experienced in your relationship with your mate? How have you resolved them?

10. How did your parents and siblings resolve conflict? How has it influenced your conflict handling style?

9
Money Matters
Counting the Cost

Don't marry for money, you can borrow it cheaper. (Scottish Proverb)

Those who love money will never have enough. How meaningless to think that wealth brings true happiness! (Ecclesiastes 5:10 NLT)

A young woman wrote in a business website: "I am a spectacularly beautiful 25-year old. I'm articulate and classy. I'm looking to (marry) a guy who makes at least half a million a year. Where do you rich single men hang out?"

She also wanted to know how men decided between "Marriage versus just a girlfriend. I am looking for MARRIAGE ONLY," she said.

In response, a man who claimed to meet her financial requirements said that from his perspective, her offer was a lousy business deal. "What you suggest is a simple trade: you bring your looks to the party, and I bring my money," he wrote. "But here's the rub: Your looks will fade and my money will continue to grow. So in economic terms you are a depreciating asset, and I am an earning asset."

"This is why," the man explained, "it does not make good business sense to 'buy you' (which is what you are asking), so I'd rather lease. So a deal that makes sense (to me) is dating, not marriage. If you want to enter into some sort of lease (agreement)," he finished up, "let me know."

Well, that was pretty harsh! But plenty of readers thought she deserved it. She was turning marriage into an economic transaction —reducing what should be a sacred relationship into nothing more than a contract and that can be a dangerous mistake. Money is an important aspect of life together in a marriage, but it should not be measured in financial terms only.

Money comes and goes. It should not and cannot form or act as a foundation of a healthy marriage relationship. Marriage should be built on a more sure foundation and not on an illusion of money, richness, material wealth and glamor. Marital research has repeatedly shown that money is a major cause of arguments in marriage and one of the top reasons for divorce. Money can create severe misunderstandings and can cripple a relationship before you know it. Talking honestly about financial matters before and during marriage will help you forge a lasting union.

> *If we fail to plan, we plan to fail.*

After making your own money decisions for many years, pooling finances with someone else can be a source of anxiety. Perhaps even more troubling is the prospect of combining incomes and filing a joint tax return. Decide how you're going to handle your financial affairs before you tie the knot and you'll find love flourish stronger. It's more complicated now than ever, but you also can access a lot of expert advice. Although marriage and money can be a stressful combination, open communication and education can help make it easier.

Some of you come from homes where finances were never discussed openly, while your future mate's home everyone knew how much everyone else earned. Some of you are spendthrifts, while your partner may be frugal. Some of you came from a low risk environment, while your mate might hail from risky financial dealings on a regular basis. Some may come from single income home, and your mate comes from dual income home. All such differences can also create significant tension in your marriage.

In a marriage, there is no "my money" and "your money" or "my debts" and "your debts." There is only "our money and our debts." A couple cannot be **one** if they separate their lives by separating their finances. God will bring a couple closer if, from the very beginning, they establish God's Word as their financial guide and then follow those principles. Couples should avoid having separate financial deals including checking accounts, because when they develop a "his money/her money" philosophy, it usually leads to a "him-versus-her" mentality. Unwillingness to join all assets and bank accounts after marriage is perhaps a danger signal that unresolved trust issues could still be lingering or developing in the relationship.

> *The rich rule over the poor, and the borrower is servant to the lender.*
> *– Proverbs 22:7*

Add Up: More Than Mere Numbers

Communicating about personal finances isn't just about exchanging numbers and putting together a budget. We all have personalities when it comes to money, our spending habits, our views on family finances, saving and fiscal planning, and sometimes even insecurities about our financial standing or history. A good offensive strategy to avoid conflicts with your money personalities is to spend some time talking about your experiences and philosophies on finances to get a better understanding of the background each person is coming from.

When we say family finances, it includes our attitude towards wealth, a proper understanding of stewardship and planning for our future. Specifically it deals with how we handle debts, income options, expenditure styles, saving, investment, assets, insurance, retirement plans, will and giving. You must also reflect on your parents' financial dealings, scriptural teaching on money management and together discuss financial goals for your household.

Seek the help of a financial planner or a banker/consultant to work through your specific financial issues and how it could affect your marriage. In case of personal or business bankruptcy, divorce/child custody or gambling is involved seek professional help. Also, in cases of inheritance and large personal assets, it would be worthwhile to discuss them at length with your future mate. Total financial disclosure with your mate will help you begin your marriage on strong footing.

Looking Back: Financial History

Whether we talk openly about family finances or not, good or poor financial habits and attitudes get rubbed on to us more than we are aware. We have seen young couples having no financial discipline, secretive about money matters and not knowing where to turn for advice in matters of their financial problems. Our attitude towards education, working hard, being honest, not spending more than what you earn, saving, staying out of debt and let your money work for you, are more acquired from our parents or older siblings. Subconsciously we emulate their habits or consciously try to reverse them.

Did you receive pocket money when you were a kid? How much did you get? What did you spend it on? How were you taught to save (piggy bank)? When did you start your first bank account? What kind of job did you do outside of your home and how much did you make? How much did money factor in your career choice? What were your motivations to save or give? What does money mean to you, buying power, security or prestige? If you were to get a million dollars as inheritance or stocks, what would you do with it? Are you used to expecting expensive gifts?

As much as possible, after marriage a couple should try to avoid getting financial assistance from their parents. It can create an unhealthy dependency and awkward situations that you won't know how to handle. It gives room for misunderstanding and comes in the way of your relationship. Sever the financial umbilical cord for the sake of your marriage.

Spending: Cash Flow & Budget

Though they may not be fun to create, budgets are an essential tool if you want to get your spending under control. The key to successful budgeting is spending less than you earn. A cash flow analysis is the first step in determining whether or not your spending is "out of control" and if you need to create a budget to rein it in. A successful budget will give you greater control of your money and help keep stay on track to reaching your financial goals.

> *Our achievements of today are but the sum total of our thoughts of yesterday. You are today where the thoughts of yesterday have brought you and you will be tomorrow where the thoughts of today take you.*
> *– Blaise Pascal*

Evaluate your personal spending details over the last few months and share it with your future mate. Your cash flow analysis shows how you spend money on a daily and monthly basis. To determine your cash flow, you should: A) Track your spending for several weeks. Record every dime you spend—both how much and what it was for. Don't just record withdrawals for cash, but record what that cash was spent on. You should be able to account for everything. B) Gather receipts. Organize the receipts for all of the expenses you've been tracking. Be sure to include your credit card bills and checkbook register for the last few months. C) Total your monthly income and expenses. Begin to add up all of your tracked expenses as well as your monthly income.

This exercise will not only help you save money but it will help you talk about your financial priorities. It will help you understand yourself and your spending habits. The next step would be to create a family budget. (See exercise at the end of the chapter).

Saving & Investing: Any Excess

Hopefully, you have some excess at the end of each month, if not individually, hopefully together you should have excess; or else it is advisable to revisit your spending list and see how you can cut expenses down in order to have a positive balance. It would be a good practice to save, even if it is a little, from your first month together. "A penny saved is a penny earned." Tiny drops do add up in marriage. All financial planners will tell you that the sooner you start saving, the more you will be able to save, so plan to start right away. If you understand how compounding principle works, you know this is true. Don't ever try to convince yourself that you can make up for not saving for a few years by saving later. It is not just the money value that matters, but the time that does the magic. You may earn more in the future, but can never make up for lost time and its compounded impact.

Some of your jobs might provide pension and retirement benefits, but in the private sector you are expected to plan for your own retirement. At twenty something, I know that retirement seems a long way off, and you probably wish I would write about how to save money on mortgages or how to use coupons at the grocery store. But this is important. Force yourself to save for retirement. Talking with your mate about life beyond career and children can itself deepen your commitment to each other and express that you are in this for the long-haul.

Debt Handling: Consolidate

One advantage Mary and I had of getting married late was that we had finished our graduate schools and had already worked for several years. We did not have any debt and had saved up some money for ourselves. But the downside was that we were very set in our ways of handling money. Fortunately, we did not have any risky financial habits, and we both shared similar values on saving and giving, but we have seen many couples struggle with their finances.

These days everyone has some level of debt burden when they get married. Whether it be car loans, educational loans, mortgage or credit cards. In marriage, both partners bring their respective debt burden into the relationship and it calls for a fresh look at handling debt henceforth. Handling the debt of two people requires a concerted effort, and it is better than doing it individually.

Joe and Jasmine had a beautiful wedding and an expensive honeymoon. Both had waited a long time and wanted to have a flashy celebration and a large party for their friends and family. Joe had changed fields and just graduated from a well-known law school. Jasmine did her undergrad in Physics and then went into an out-of-state medical school. Both had taken several student loans to complete their professional studies. She still had a few years of residency before being a "real" doctor and he was working for a government agency. In spite of a sound future, their current income was meager and together their debt was huge. They charged their wedding expenses to the credit cards and could afford only to pay the minimum monthly payments. The high interest rates on credit cards with car loans and student loan sent them spiraling downward deep in debt.

Everyone has credit cards these days. It would be a worthwhile exercise to gather all your credit and debit cards on the table and discuss them. Talk about how long you had each of those cards, current outstanding debt, usage pattern and payments made. You may want to decide which of the cards are going to be your primary household credit cards, and some you may have to cancel all together. Most financial planners recommend that cancellation of a credit card affect the individual's credit report and are not generally recommended. Some recommend that if one spouse has good credit and the other has damaged credit, it is important to not merge the bad with the good. To ensure that doesn't happen, do not put your spouse's name on any of your financial accounts. But we suggest both of you learn to share the joy and challenges of your life together, including debts and poor credit ratings.

Develop a plan to reduce debt redundancies and pay down debts. Identify areas where bills unnecessarily overlap and look for opportunities to use your married status to decrease expenses. For example, most cellular phone companies offer family plans that can cut monthly phone costs, or see if joining the same gym can help to reduce monthly dues. Learn to live within your means. Do not live life on future earnings. Develop a rainy-day fund—a sum of money that you set apart for emergencies in life—vehicle breakdown, health challenges or loss of job. Financial discipline is critical for getting out of debt and staying out of it. Having a plan to get out of debt and holding yourself accountable to someone is the secret of living debt-free.

> "Do not store up for yourselves treasures on earth, where moth and rust destroy, and where thieves break in and steal. But store up for yourselves treasures in heaven, where moth and rust do not destroy, and where thieves do not break in and steal. For where your treasure is, there your heart will be also."
> – Jesus (Matthew 6:19–21)

Giving: Good Stewardship

We need to recognize that managing money is a spiritual issue. Did you know that Jesus spoke more about money than he did about any other topic? In fact, fifteen percent of all the recorded words of Jesus are on the subject of money—more than his teachings on heaven and hell combined. God owns everything and we are entrusted a small portion and expected to be good steward of all that he has given us. Developing an attitude of gratitude for all his blessing will place all of our possession in its right place. Another virtue that can greatly deepen our marital relationship is contentment. Contrary to the hoarding that contemporary culture promotes hoarding, virtuous life calls us to be generous and provide for the less fortunate among us.

We are called to be good stewards of all that we are given. That stewardship is lived out in recognizing God as the source of all good gifts, taking those gifts—whether meager or much—giving thanks, and then offering those gifts in response to his prompting in our hearts. Recognizing marginalized people next door can fill our hearts with gratitude for the much we tend to take for granted. This is another area where you and your mate might see things differently or might have different causes that you believe in or want to support. If neither of you are in the habit of giving, this is something you could begin soon after your marriage. The joy and blessing that giving brings is something you will experience only by doing it. Indeed, it is more blessed to give than to receive. It cultivates a giving heart in us and the same attitude will flow out to each other in marriage, for marriage is more about giving than receiving any way.

Decisions: Household Financial Management

Several financial decisions lay ahead of you. Some of you might do without much thought and can create misunderstanding. Will both of you work or one stay home? Would you be a single income household or dual income? Would you work outside of the home or work from home? Whose job is banking, bookkeeping and bill payments? How will you decide on purchasing big ticket items? What are you personal discretionary expenditure limits? Who controls the finances? How many checkbooks or credit cards should you have? What are the tax implications when you get married? What would be your living standards?

Banking needs will vary depending on your situations. Some would need to keep separate accounts in different banks as before while other will need to open an entirely new joint account in a bank near your new home? There is no best solution that would work perfectly for all. You have to decide what will work best for you. Experts advise keeping separate personal accounts and opening a joint account for household expenses, particularly if you are a two-paycheck couple. Deciding how to spend the household money will keep you talking about how you want to handle your finances. Even if you decide to pool everything, it's wise to give each of you a set amount to do with as you wish to avoid conflicts. You may want to put each other's names on your separate accounts for easier access in an emergency.

> *Marriage halves our grief, doubles our joys, and quadruples our expenses.*
> *– English Proverb*

Depending on your income and tax bracket, a married couple filling jointly may owe more tax than they did when they were both single. Two working people who combine their incomes on one tax form are suddenly vaulted to a higher tax bracket than they occupied before. Consulting a tax planner in your first year of marriage will be good idea. Another related decision after marriage is what are your financial obligation towards your aging parents? Will you be paying for their needs? In case of emergency, what would you do?

Wedding Bills: Dowry & Wedding Cost

A uniquely Indian issue when it comes to marriage is dowry—money, goods, jewelry, automobile or estate that a woman brings to her new husband. Though it is officially illegal, the age-old practice is quite prevalent among Indians in rural India as well as the global diaspora. In many cases, the bride and groom might not have any say in this matter. The marriage brokers and parents would determine how much wealth exchanges hands. It has taken several different forms now—a gift from the bride's parents, land or material things (flat, car, business capital etc.).

Stories of dowry harassment and even dowry deaths are heard regularly. The social evil of this practice and the exploitation that goes on in the name of dowry can go on throughout the married life. Dowry is a favored form of female family inheritance and a method of "equalizing" with a groom of higher social status. In a patriarchal society, family wealth is shared only among boys, and girls are given dowry at their wedding to join with her husband's family.

After many years of marriage, bitterness that the groom did not get an adequate payment at his marriage sticks out as a sore thumb, and in some cases, it takes a violent turn. We suggest that the couple be involved in these conversations parents are having. You must speak your conviction on this matter and

Nothing can stop the person with the right mental attitude from achieving their goal; Nothing on earth can help the person with the wrong mental attitude.
– Thomas Jefferson

do not let financial exchange ruin the possibility of making your relationship richer. Dowry should never be demanded, and it should not be conditional to the marriage. Often times, parents are happy to share their wealth with their children, but a new relationship can never be forged based on the amount of money changing hands.

In recent years wedding costs have shot up astronomically. People spend exorbitant amount of money at their engagement and wedding ceremonies including clothes and jewelry, parties and honeymoon. The happiest day of your life can become the one that ruined your finances and credit rating for years to come. Set a budget prior to planning the wedding and stick to it! There are a lot of convenient ways to cut costs and still have a beautiful wedding.

Discuss how the wedding costs will be paid for, and include both sides of the families in the conversations. Share the burden of the entire wedding cost as equally as possible.

Financial Goals: Safety Net

You and your partner may have strong ideas about your financial goals for the future whether it is buying a house, getting a new car, investing heavily for retirement or preparing for children. It is important to discuss these goals so that you can both be on the same page and develop a financial plan that represents both of your interests. Remember, compromise is an important part of any marriage's financial plan. Work together to set goals that compliment your individual desires as well as your future household. With your financial goals decided, it is important to be fiscally responsible and put a plan in place to meet those goals and get closer to your dreams for the future.

Exercise 9a: Couple's First Budget

Income per Month			Marriage Budget
	His	Hers	Ours
Salary			
Other Income (interest, dividends, etc.)			
Gross Income			
Then subtract:			
Charitable giving			
Savings			
Others			
Total Income			
Expense per month			
Housing: Rent/Mortgage/ Lease Insurance Taxes Miscellaneous (repairs etc)			

Utilities: Electricity Gas Water Phone (landline & cell) Cable/Television Internet Trash Other			
Food: Groceries Eating out Other			
Auto: Payment/Lease Fuel Repairs Replacement Other			
Medical: Doctor Dentist Pharmacy Other			
Insurance: Life Health Auto Other			

	His	Hers	Ours
Debt: Education Credit/Debit Card _____ _____ _____ _____			
Housing Loans Auto loans Personal (friends/ family) Other			
Entertainment: Movie Vacation Sports/Gym Other			
Clothing: New purchase Dry cleaning			
Miscellaneous: Beauty/Barber Toiletries Furniture Newspaper/ Magazine Subscriptions Gifts Emergencies Gym/Club membership Gardening Hobbies Online payments			

Total expenses:			
Total Income			
Less total expenses			
Balance:			

Exercise 9b: Financial Disclosures

Investments	His	Her	Ours
Securities, stocks, bonds			
Insurance policies			
Retirement accounts			
Expected Inheritances			
Rain-day fund			
Petty cash			
Tax bracket			
Personal Lending			
Credit Card limits_____ _____ _____			
Assets Land Home Automobile Personal properties (furniture, computers) Others			
Total savings in bank accounts			
Jewelry			
Wedding Costs			
Wills/Trusts			
Volunteering commitments			
Others			

Exercise 9c: Financial History

1. What were the financial status of your parents (poor, middle class or wealthy)? Define the terms as well. Did both of them work outside of home? How much did they earn?

2. What values about money did you learn from your parents?

3. What stands out in your mind about your parents' habits (earning, spending, saving, giving and investing)? Did they plan for future, retirement, your education and marriage?

4. What financial habits of your parents would you like to emulate and what you would like to avoid?

5. What lessons on money management have you learned from your family or extended relatives?

6. Mark everything that applies to your parents and discuss with your mate its details:

o Cutting coupons	o Setting financial goals
o Shopped for best deals in town	o Miserly/Stingy/Frugal
o Paying bills on time	o Gambling
o Lending to friends/family	o Use credit cards
o Invest in stocks and bonds	o Overspending
o Generous to poor and needy	o Keeping up with neighbors
o Bankruptcy is ok	o Work hard/overtime
o Laid off from work	o Unemployed/ Out of business
o Use online banking/bill pay	o Shop for cheapest deals
o Shopped only name brand items	o Work on cash basis
o Inherited wealth, land or other valuables	o Careless with money
o Gave to charity or religious causes	o Have debt
o Provided for their parents or siblings	o Impulsive shopper
o Worry about future	o "God owns it all" attitude
o Gift giving	o Kept good records
o Conservative or aggressive in investing	o Paying full or minimum on credit cards
o	
o	
o	

Exercise 9d: Financial Goals

1. Write down the financial goals that you would like to achieve during the next three years.

a. _____

b. _____

c. _____

d. _____

e. _____

f. _____

g. _____

2. From the list of goals you just made, pick the five most important short and long-term financial goals that you want to accomplish.

3. Make these goals as specific, measurable, and attainable as possible (so you will know exactly what you're aiming for and when you've achieved it).

4. Identify what immediate action you can take within the next 48 hours to take your first step.

5. Think of a couple of steps you need to take to further your action plan.

6. Determine the date you would like to achieve this goal.

10

Sex Matters
Getting Intimate

Love is a matter of chemistry, but sex is a matter of physics. (Unknown)

Marriage should be honored by all, and the marriage bed kept pure.
(Hebrews 13:4a)

"What is wrong with that?" asked Vinod, a young man who had been meeting regularly to talk about relationship issues. Vinod is in a relationship with Vimala for over a year, more seriously over last two months. They are thinking of getting engaged soon.

Today our conversation narrowed down on sex. He feels they are in a serious relationship and sex should be okay. "We are going to get married within months. So why can't we express love to each other in a deep manner. It will seal our relationship, right?"

He continued his argument, "In fact, she wants it too. So do I. We both are consensual partners and we are committed to each other. So what is wrong?"

"But...," he paused.

"But what?" I enquired.

"She said she does not want to get pregnant before the wedding and that we should take precautionary measures to avoid any further complication as a result of it."

"Umm…. so what have you both decided?" I asked.

Vinod calmly replied, "I want to do it. Otherwise she will think I do not love her or am committed to her. We will have 'safe sex' to allay her fears. But I am not sure if it is right. That's why I want to talk to you. Will it affect our relationship in future?"

People are in serious quandary when it comes to sexual matters. They are constantly bombarded with a plethora of divergent sexual values and are confused about the whole issue. Parents and cultures consider it a taboo. Popular media, school and peers have often advocated a permissive view in this regard. A proper perspective on sexuality with the view of marriage is drowned in the sea of destructive viewpoints.

> *First, Is it a good thing to have sexual relations? Certainly—but only within a certain context. It's good for a man to have a wife, and for a woman to have a husband. Sexual drives are strong, but marriage is strong enough to contain them and provide for a balanced and fulfilling sexual life in a world of sexual disorder.*
> *– Paul (1 Corinthians 7:1, 2 MSG)*

Designer's View: Oneness

God created sex. It is one of the greatest gifts that God has given married couples. Sex in a marriage offers two people one of the most powerful ways to express their love for each other. Sex with all its pleasures, drives, potentials and dangers were in the mind of God when he first created human beings. It was not an afterthought and God was not unaware of its potential misuse. Human beings were created as sexual beings even before the Fall. Though distinct in their sexuality, both men and women are created in God's image. Unlike the rest of the creation, we hold in us a capacity to relate one another deeply, and sexual union can create an intimate bond unlike any other. The creation accounts say, *"The man and his wife were both naked and felt no shame"* (Genesis 2:25). They did not get any sex education or have any "How To" manuals. They simply knew how to be intimate with each other.

Sex is sacred. According to the Creator's design sex came with boundaries within the confines of marriage and intended to cultivate intimacy in marriage, provide pleasure and used for procreation. It was God's plan and he established certain parameters namely, marriage, to protect and maximize our experience of getting intimate. When we ignore the original design, we often reap a harvest of pain and suffering. We honor God both by participating in sex with our spouse and refraining from it with anyone else.

God has drawn a firm line against casual and illicit sex. There is no place for polygamy, adultery, incest, same-sex, prostitution or bestiality and other sexual deviations. The original design confines sex within an exclusive committed relationship between a husband and his wife. Sex has never been only about the physical act, but has the potential to unite bodies, emotions and spirits. All three is necessary and we cannot become one with many.

Taboo Topic

In many traditional homes and cultures, people shy from talking openly about sex. It is considered a private topic and even married couple feels awkward to talk about it. On the contrary, popular media and obscence expressions are bursting with sexual slangs. Though this topic is a taboo, sex is everywhere—television, advertisements, catalogs, curse words, locker room, books and internet are ripe with its usage. There are no age-appropriate, organized and systematic approaches to exposing kids to a healthy view on sex. Distorted information and attitudes on sexuality often get widely disseminated.

Many consider sex as bad or dirty. Not to be talked about openly, but only to be engaged for procreation. Some cultures stamp it as a taboo topic while some faiths permit a lenient promiscuous approach to it. Many adults and youth leaders do not know how to talk about this comfortably. Most people blush red when the word "sex" is mentioned out loud. For most people in their growing up years, sex wasn't talked about very much; not at home, not with family, and certainly not in religious gatherings! The lack of correct information inspires intrigue and sex becomes even more appealing for teens and young adults. The lure of the unknown consumes the mind, and much like Eve, regret ensues after one taste of the forbidden fruit.

Some consider the bounds of marriage as limiting and want to experiment with sex without any commitment. Hooking up is the new way among young singles, which leads to one night stands.

> *Flee the evil desires of youth, and pursue righteousness, faith, love and peace, along with those who call on the Lord out of a pure heart.*
>
> *– Paul (2 Timothy 2:22)*

First Impressions

Our early attitudes toward sex tend to stick with us for a long time. Do you remember where, when and from whom, you first heard about sex? Where did your attitudes about sex come from? Was it parents, friends, teachers, siblings, television/movie, books/magazines, pornography or internet?

You may have come from a home where there was no mention of the topic. Hearing anything about sex from the media or friends, you might feel a strange sense of curiosity wanting to know more about it. On the other hand, you may have received instruction on sex appropriately from your parent from very early age. Your same gender parent may have given you the first sex-talk and you may have a healthy view of masculinity and femininity and may have shielded you from talking about sexual issues over dinner table.

If you and your mate come from these two polarized homes

in matters of sexual attitudes, you will have much work to do. You must talk with each other about the unhealthy things you learned or experienced in your family. Did dirty jokes or pornographic images find its way in your childhood home?

Prakash accidently ran into a "girlie" website at his college computer lab. He kept revisiting those sites and started downloading nude female images and videos. The images got riveted in his mind quickly and pretty much shaped this young man's view of woman's body and sexual activities. It became habitual to spend hours on porn sites watching adult videos. By the time he got married to Priya, he was addicted to online pornography and his unhealthy habit continued after their marriage as well. One day she caught him watching a porn video online at home. He made a few futile attempts to deny his pornography addiction, but on the face of Priya's unrelenting insistence, he finally confessed. She

> The truth is whenever a man lies with a woman, whether they like it or not, a transcended relation is set up between them, which must be eternally enjoyed or eternally endured.
> – C.S. Lewis, The Screwtape Letters

felt betrayed and that her husband wasn't sexually fulfilled with her. The sexual dysfunction, distrust and heartache began to cause a rift in their relationship and it wasn't long before their marriage fell apart. Having been separated from Priya, Prakash realized the price of his addiction and decided to seek help. He hopes to get clean and reclaim his broken trust and marriage to Priya.

Rani recently got engaged and was busy planning for her wedding. She was fearful how she would talk about her sexual past to her fiancé. She was molested and sexually abused as a child by a close relative. The shame of the experience led to a promiscuous lifestyle in college. The fear of rejection kept her from sharing about it with premarital counselors and even her future husband. She thought the secrets would die with her, but it began to surface in the marriage. Her husband got frustrated and the marriage is in crisis after crisis. She now realized that she should have gotten counseling before the marriage and should have told everything to her husband. Now she wonders how she would respond if he asks "why didn't you tell me all these years?"

Schools and media are other major sources of information on sex. You might have had regular sex education classes from teachers or conversation with peers in locker rooms, been exposed to "safe sex" campaign materials. As a result you may have picked up a wide range of attitudes towards sex like mutually consenting sex is okay, always use contraceptives, condom usage protects against STDs and AIDS, viewing porn is fine, coarse joking, oral sex, and public display of affection is acceptable. All of these attitudes towards sex in the formative years are critical in shaping our views on sex and marital intimacy. All good and bad values that we learn from others are crucial in developing our own value system. Talk with each other

> *Blessed are the pure in heart, for they will see God.*
> *– Jesus (Matthew 5:8)*

about some of your views on sexuality and why you feel the way you do.

Purity: Unadulterated Pleasure

Purity is God's order when it comes to sex, both before and after the wedding. Abstinence before marriage and fidelity within marriage is the divine order. Human sexual drive finds its full expression within the bounds of marriage—an exclusive committed relationship between a man and a woman for a lifetime. The designer of sex knew that we would require a lifetime to master the art of becoming one without any trace of contamination. The pseudo-thrill of different partners quickly fades when compared with the excitement of physically connecting with the one person who knows you better than anyone else on earth. Sex within marriage allows us to experience communication, companionship and comprehension at the deepest level possible. It keeps us from seeking sexual release elsewhere and prepares us for holy living. This act can bring a new life into the world and we become part of God's creative work in creating a brand new being.

If you are single, we would urge you to abstain from sexual activity until you are married. Take a vow to be sexually abstinent and hold yourself accountable in this area. If you are in a relationship or engaged and are sexually active with your fiancé(e), we would exhort you to refrain from sexual activity right away. Seek forgiveness from God and your partner. If you are not yet married and are living together, we would encourage one of you to move out. You may use this time until marriage to get to know each other without sexual involvement. Several studies have proven how premarital sex and cohabitation reduce the chances of marital success and true intimacy.

> *Though you have made me see troubles, many and bitter, you will restore my life again; from the depths of the earth, you will again bring me up.*
> *– Psalm 71:20*

The recent researches in social sciences suggest that living together is not a good way to prepare for marriage or to avoid divorce. Cohabitation is detrimental to successful relationships for adults and especially harmful for children. Cohabiting unions tend to weaken the institution of marriage and pose clear dangers for women and children. Living together before marriage increases the risk of divorce. Living together outside marriage increases the risk of domestic violence for women and the risk of physical and sexual abuse for children. Unmarried couples have lower levels of happiness and well-being than married couples. Serial or multiple short-term cohabitations are detrimental to future relational stability. Women experience a disproportional percentage of the negative aspects of cohabitation.

Purity should not be limited to sexual acts, but also thoughts and one's inner life. Sexual purity is violated in thoughts that may never manifest in outward acts. Sex must never be used to oppress, wrong or take advantage of anyone. Rape, incest, sexual abuse, pedophilia, voyeurism, prostitution and pornography always exploit and corrupt.

Healing from Sexual Pasts

Many bring their past sexual exploits into their marriage. Whether you simply fooled around, had sex or were molested or raped, your sexual past does affect your relationship. The loss of virginity can cause a sense of guilt, feeling dirty or used, create fear of intimacy, expose to sexually transmitted diseases and incite comparison with past sexual partners. In cases of promiscuity, it can put flashbacks or pop-ups in the mind of that person that can significantly interfere with intimate moments in the marriage relationship. In the cases of abuse, it can taint or even eliminate the

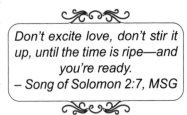

Don't excite love, don't stir it up, until the time is ripe—and you're ready.
– Song of Solomon 2:7, MSG

physical pleasure because of the mental and emotional associations with intimate touch. In cases, where there were conceptions and abortions involved, it can create real complications in your marriage.

Concerning the person who has a sexual history, whether it is the man or woman, this greatly affects intimacy with your spouse. Confessing your moral failure with your mate is important, without going into all graphic details of your sexual history. Also be prepared to listen to your mate's sexual failures and be willing to accept him/her as he/she is and extend grace. If past experiences are affecting your sexual relationship, don't hesitate to seek assistance from a professional counselor who has helped others with similar struggles. By God's grace, healing is possible and you must seek to whole again before committing to enter into a relationship or marriage.

We believe, no matter what your sexual past had been, you can be whole again and experience fullness within marriage. Healing and recovering from past sexual abuse or "sexperimentations" is an important aspect of preparing for marriage.

Marital Sex: Looking Forward

After the wedding, one of the hardest things for young couples to adjust to is the fact that sex is suddenly okay! All the years of silence on the "forbidden topic," feeling guilty of asking questions, wondering and dreaming, thinking sex as a four letter word, suddenly diminish. Now sex is permitted, expected, to be enjoyed and not only that, but it's a part of God's plan! Before the wedding you kept hearing that one should abstain from sex and after the wedding you are supposed to do it. Such thinking creates a false sense of guilt, a shamed self and develops insecurity.

If you are getting married soon, it would be appropriate to discuss sexual intimacy with your mate, without actually trying it. After you are married, you will have the joy of knowing each other on a much deeper level. Avoid the temptation to engage in it prematurely and rob the excitement of being intimate with each other on your wedding night. Seek to please each other and keep the interest of your mate above your own. Get one or two of the books mentioned under recommended reading during the honeymoon and read it together. Overcome your natural inhibition and cultural biases to freely express yourself sexually to each other. Gain understanding of differences in male–female sexuality, passion and needs. Love making is a lifelong learning experience; do not jump to conclusions based on your initial experience. Be vulnerable to each other and talk about your experiences. Sex is a deeply private thing, between a husband and wife. One partner may value its privacy more than the other, and hence, it is important to respect each other's feelings.

Sex isn't a reward or a game, and it's not something to withhold as a punishment. The apostle Paul tells couples: *Do not deprive each other [of sex] except by mutual consent and for a time, so that you may devote yourselves to prayer. Then come together again. . .* (1 Corinthians 7:5). Give yourself freely to each other, and do not force it on your mate. Frequency and variety is something you both have to decide based on your lifestyle and needs.

You will experience your greatest sexual intimacy with one person. That's the person with whom you also share emotional, intellectual and spiritual intimacy, the covenant of marriage and a strong commitment to God. No other sexual pleasure compares to that experienced by a husband and wife who feel safe with each other at all levels of their lives. So if you want great sex in your marriage, work on your relationship, and on communicating your love to each other. It's also important to deal with conflict as it arises. If there's any unresolved conflict in a relationship, it can keep a couple from fully enjoying the sexual aspect of their marriage.

Exercise 10a: Getting Intimate

Reflect and write down answers to the questions below. Do the first half individually and the rest as a couple. If you are not comfortable, you do not have to share with each other. But be completely honest in reflecting and answering these questions. Write down your answers on a separate sheet, journal or on a computer.

Individually:

1. What was your family's attitude towards sex?

2. How did you first learn about sex?

3. What experiences and influences from your childhood and adolescence might hinder healthy sex with your mate?

4. How well do you know about the physiology of your own body and the opposite gender?

5. Are you comfortable talking about sex? Why or why not?

6. How have parents, media, peers and popular culture shaped your view of sex?

7. How comfortable are you with your body? Appearance, beauty, shape, private parts?

8. Did you have any sexual fantasy or engage in sexual experimentation?

9. What were your reactions to sexual jokes or watching pornographic content for the first time?

10. Did you masturbate (self-stimulation)? When did you start? How did you learn about it? How did you feel about it?

As a couple:

1. On a scale of one to five (one being the least important and five being the most important), how important is sex to you in marriage?

2. What worries do you have about sex?

3. Who initiates sex?

4. How frequently do you expect to have sex in marriage?

5. How will you know if your mate wants sex or just closeness?

6. What is your attitude toward giving and receiving sexual pleasure?

7. What are unacceptable sexual acts or behaviors for you?

8. What would ruin sexual intimacy for you?

9. What would make sex act really great for you?

10. What do you do if your mate does not want sex (not in a mood) or your mate wants it "all the time"?

Exercise 10b: Sexual Integrity Covenant

With the authority of the Father, in the power of Jesus' blood, and under the direction of the Holy Spirit, I, _____, am establishing a covenant with God regarding my sexual life.

I promise I will stay sexually pure until I get married and remain faithful to my wife/husband thereafter. I refrain from giving in to sexual temptation or any sexual immorality in my life.

I admit that I battle with sexual temptation; therefore, I commit to being victorious according to God's standard of sexual integrity —that in me there must not be even a hint of sexual immorality (Ephesians 5:3).

I will pray daily that God would grant me victory with respect to my eyes, my surroundings, my mind, my heart and my body.

1. I will divert my eyes from and starve them of sexually charged sights.

   "I made a covenant with my eyes not to look lustfully at a girl" *(Job 31:1).*

2. I will avoid situations that have a potential for sexual temptation
   Flee from sexual immorality (1 Corinthians 6:18a).

3. I will not tolerate any sexually impure thoughts.
   We take captive every thought to make it obedient to Christ (2 Corinthians 10:5b).

4. I will cherish God far above sexual gratification.
   But in your hearts set apart Christ as Lord (1 Peter 3:15).

5. I will dedicate my body to God and his work.
   You were bought at a price. Therefore honor God with your body (1 Corinthians 6:20).

I will memorize the above five Bible verses within a month of signing this covenant.

I will find at least one same gender accountability partner with whom I will be honest about my sexual temptations within a month of signing this covenant.

The instant that I find I have succumb to sexual temptation, I will confess my sin to God immediately and ask for forgiveness. I will be transparent to my fiancé(e)/spouse of the sexual struggles and weakness. I will not conceal my sexual sins from God and my mate.

_____   _____

Signature   Date

Faith Matters
Believing in the Maker of Marriage

My husband and I divorced over religious differences. He thought he was God, and I didn't. (Unknown)

When a woman marries, the law binds her to her husband as long as he is alive. (Romans 7:2a TLB)

Ishan and Isabel were polar opposites but drawn to each other. Their personalities, outlooks on life, and worldviews were dramatically different. She grew up in America, a second generation Malayalee Christian and he from a Muslim background grew up in North India, a graduate student in an American university. They met at the college student body meeting. Both were in the same department and gradually fell in love. She had a large family of uncles, aunts and cousins an hour away from campus. He was alone in America, in fact, he was the first one from his family to pursue college education or go overseas. Rest of the family in India was anxiously waiting for their only son to return after American education and take care of all family obligations, including arranging the marriage of his three sisters. He wanted her to convert to Islam and raise their kids as Muslim. She would have to live in India wearing veil. She could never think of returning to rural India and began persuading him to settle in America. As their upbringings, cultural and religious differences, vision for the future began to collide, they realized both would be better off without the other and decide to break up their long cherished love affair, with much heartache.

Faith plays a crucial role in shaping our values, character and outlook on life. Differences in belief systems, spirituality and practices are bound to make the marital bond difficult. The very core of any marriage is a profound sense of union between a man and woman which includes spiritual and not merely emotional, relational and sexual. Moreover, the divine power that keeps a couple together for life and letting them reach the highest potential of marriage is indispensible in building a lasting and fulfilling marriage.

> *A cord of three strands is not quickly broken. (Ecclesiastes 4:12)*

Designer's View: Cord of Three

Christian marriage is not simply the union of two people, but of three. By the way, third person is not the mother-in-law! God should be the third person in the marriage. The one who saw Adam's loneliness and created Eve as his life partner and who instituted marriage in the garden of Eden wants to be active in our marriages. Not coming in our way, but helping us grow in greater mutuality and to become one, as he has designed marriage to be. Adam and Eve had no earthly parents. Their allegiance was first to God and then to each other, under God.

Marriage is not a two-dimensional relationship, but a three-dimensional one. The Creator of marriage is the third dimension and provides the much needed stability. It is akin to the three legs of a stool. Two selfish people could pull the marriage in different directions and it can only go separate ways. But a third person —

who is selfless, all loving and giving, who has the best interest of the couple with no ulterior motives, can bring steadiness when marriage comes under strain. When the third person is God himself, there is much hope for oneness in marriage. God not only knows how marriage is supposed to be, but wants to play an active role in helping us realize his greater dreams for our lives together in marriage. The closer that you get to God, the closer you get to each other.

God is still in the business of creating marriages. He desires to be the foundation stone of each union. Most marriages are based on nothing; it isn't surprising that many collapse. But, it's never too late with God. At any point, if we turn over our lives and our marriages to him, he will become the foundation, the builder, and the rebuilder, if that's necessary, of that home. Even the broken pieces of our lives can be mended and repaired if we let God be God in every area of our human relationships.

Marriage is sacred. Faith and spirituality is an integral part of marriage and family life. Marriage has spiritual core and helps us grow in every facet of life. Marriage helps us draw close to God and have a strong relationship with God first, and making that the basis of building a strong relationship with your mate. The stronger your relationship with God and the closer you feel toward him, same will be reflected in your marriage relationship. Marriage was intended to make us holy than to make us happy. It also helps us to trust God more fully and to love him more dearly. Every aspect of married life holds the potential to discover and reveal more of God. In fact, a strong and stable marriage brings God closer to the world around us. Marriage aids us to transform into Christlikeness and molds Christ's character in us. Marriage, the way God designed it, is meant to draw people to God. The family is God's laboratory where his grace and provision are put to the test. It helps to beat the selfishness out of us.

Belief and behaviors are intertwined. Our convictions about life, values, and morality are formed by our belief system. How we relate to each other and think about others are considerably fashioned by our worldview, which is shaped by our belief system. Faith inspired values help us not only to endure but grow and thrive. Values that are tested and proven over time are those build on unchanging divine precepts.

Interfaith: Mixed Marriages

Interfaith marriages are unavoidable. History and common sense show us that it is inevitable in modern, secular and multicultural societies. In rural places, interreligious marriages may be objectionable, but in cities and among Asian Indians abroad, intermarriages are becoming very common. As young people interact across languages, cultures, races and faiths in colleges, workplaces, neighborhoods and now over the internet, they are enchanted by differing backgrounds, and are falling in love and getting married. This trend is only bound to increase. However, mixed marriages are not easy at all and tend to bring unique challenges to the relationship. There is a relatively higher percentage of interfaith marriages breaking than same faith couples.

> *God designed marriage to make us holy more than to make us happy.*
> *– Gary Thomas*

Another difficulty such couples face is absence of a peer group. No matter where they go, whether his or her community, they tend to stick out. They can never feel fully understood and people are always critical and judgmental towards them. When kids come along, things become even more complicated. To which faith will the kids adhere? How will parents divide their time between each of their parents and faith obligations? Beyond the lure of a new faith, the inability to find others like them isolates them in the society and causes loneliness.

Some advocate that faith is a matter of choice and love between couples should be strong enough to allow each partner to practice the faiths of his/her choice. The lack of spiritual commonality is sure to bring a great deal of confusion in interfaith marriages and even more confusion for the next generation. A couple may agree to practice two different faith systems, without treading into each other's territories but it is difficult to remain intellectually honest about the contradictory belief systems. We know of a couple who goes to a Hindu temple with their kids on Saturday and to the church on Sunday mornings. These interfaith couples are carving out a new spirituality and a social change, but never seriously considered claims of both of their faith systems.

Religion has always had a strong interest in the family, because families were seen as the way in which the next generation would be socialized and taught the traditions of the religious communities. If parents are against intermarriage, the stage is set for conflict, bitterness and misunderstanding, with damaging and long-lasting consequences for these relationships. The larger faith community also tends to ostracize interfaith couples and without a meaningful support group, making marriage work alone can be burdensome.

> *Choose for yourselves this day whom you will serve. . .But as for me and my household, we will serve the LORD.*
> *– Joshua 24:15.*

We are not talking about intercaste or interracial marriage here. We believe such marriage can thrive if they have foundational spiritual commonality. With a common God as a cementing force, no matter how different your race, color, caste, denominational or backgrounds may be, you still can build a strong and lasting marriage. Such marriages do come with its own unique challenges and would be much harder than for couples from similar cultures and backgrounds. Nonetheless, intercultural marriages bring unique richness and depth of understanding that are commonly not found in mono-cultural marriages. Studies have shown that strong genuine faith is connected with strong family life. Interfaith marriages tend to divide the home right at its very core.

God disciples us through our marriage. Marriage is an ideal

crucible in which God wants to transform us into the likeness of Jesus Christ. God uses our mate to shape character and virtues in us. Keeping God central in your marriage takes effort and it is nearly impossible when the husband and wife worship two different gods. If you feel the need to spice up your marriage, make sure you don't leave out the most essential ingredient, faith. If you have relied on merely psychological tools and insights to build a strong marriage, you will find it wanting. Faith and spirituality are often overlooked aspects in relational health and fulfillment. Secular approaches are insufficient and we must draw deeply from our faith reservoirs.

To believe in the first institution and its Creator requires faith. Personal piety, a small group of peers for learning, support and accountability, a communal worship, serving and giving opportunities are crucial in building strong and lasting marriages. The timeless principles of the Scriptures and an affirming community are indispensable ingredients to the marriage building process. It's becoming increasingly clear that strong families depend on churches, and churches depend on strong families.

Marriage also exposes the weakness in an individual and in your mate's life. We are not perfect people, although it might seem like that before the marriage. When you begin to live your life in an intimate setting like that of marriage, you come to realize how self-centered you are. It only proves the need for a savior, who can help us to look outward at others needs instead of inward at our own needs. We need to be selfless by becoming other centered, making a priority to meet first the needs of our mates, even if our own needs are not met. Faith acts like glue in binding two people in marriage. Faith is a strong adhesive that holds two people together. Dissimilar faiths do not create necessary glue required for lasting marriage. It tends to pull the couple in different directions. Also, without faith aspects, marriage will fail to serve the greater purposes God intended.

Unequally Yoked: Coupling

Tara is a Christian girl in her mid twenties and a science teacher in a local middle school. She was in a serious relationship with a Hindu boy. She wanted to talk more about their relationship and how she could get her parents to agree with her decision. Both parents were opposed to the relationship since they had known about it.

"Why can't I marry him? Why do my parents disapprove of my choice?"

"So, what are your parents saying?" I inquired.

"Nothing more than 'you can't marry a Hindu.' I kept asking why and they do not have any answer." she replied. "He is such a nice boy," she said, "better than many of the 'Christians' I see at church. Why are my parents so opposed to it?"

Before I asked her anything she continued, "He is educated, has a good job, comes from a nice family. What more could one want? The only thing my parents are against is that he is from a Hindu family. Neither of us is heavily into religious stuff, anyway. Why are my parents bent on his religious background?"

When she paused to catch her breath, I shot some questions at her, "Where will you be married? Why do you think marrying someone from similar religious background is so important to your parents? In which faith will you raise your kids? I mean, will you take them to church or a temple?"

"I do not know. I haven't planned out the rest of my life. I love him, and he loves me. I know we will be happy together." After thoughtful deliberation she asked me, "Does the Bible say anything about marrying a Hindu?"

Knowing this was going to be a long conversation I asked, "Have you read 2 Corinthians 6:14?" She fumbled through her Bible to find the passage, and read it aloud, *Be ye not unequally yoked together with unbelievers: for what fellowship hath righteousness with unrighteousness? And what communion hath light with darkness?* What does that mean?

Spiritual beliefs and maturity really matters in marriage. Mere feelings are not enough to keep two people together for life. Interfaith marriages are unequal coupling, no matter how emotionally, intellectually, and socially compatible you are. Paul's warning to Corinthian believers was not to get "bound" with unbelievers. Though it did not refer to marriage particularly, many have extrapolated the principle to marital union as well. The imagery is drawn from Old Testament Law which forbade harnessing an ox and an ass, a clean and an unclean beast, together to a plow. Paul uses this passage in a figurative way: the believer has been cleansed; the unbeliever refuses to be cleansed. What business do they have under the same yoke?

Nowhere in the Bible will one find a command, "Thou shall not marry a non-Christian." In fact, there are several references in the Bible of such unions. Paul, in 1 Corinthians 7:12–16, speaks to those who are married to unbelievers, encouraging them to stay together, working to bring their partners to a saving relationship with Jesus Christ. The apostle Peter also encourages wives of unbelievers to work to win their husbands to the Lord (1 Peter 3:1, 2). Obviously, religiously mixed marriages are not the absolute. There are serious problems involved with such unions and many are destined to fail. Nevertheless, they do exist, and Christians who find themselves in such circumstances should do their best to bring a positive influence to those relationships.

In a close and intimate relationship like that of marriage, a Christ–follower should seek the companionship of another Christ–follower only. This way, both would help and encourage each other in the service of God. Both could live beyond themselves to a greater kingdom cause. Moreover, it is the duty of Christian parents to rear their children in the nurture and admonition of the Lord. How can one do this when one spouse's religious belief differ? Scripture certainly forbids persons tying themselves down to unbelievers in any business or any relation by which the believer is influenced or controlled by the unbeliever. It is more critical in the area of marriage than any other.

Faith & Family: Support System

Marriage is not simply about two individuals, but is the coming together of two families. Interfaith marriages create a lot of complicated scenarios when you consider the family of origin, extended relatives and community. Negotiating parental expectations, wedding rituals, conflicting values, and traditions are not going to be easy. Families are best nurtured and sustained in a faith community.

Some renounce the faith of their family in order to join the faith of their mate and get married according to its customs. Some go through the motions of both religious traditions like getting married both in Hindu temple and Christian church. Some abdicate both and choose to have a private civil ceremony or court marriage and have a joint public reception party. But no matter what route you take, not everyone will be happy with your decision. It is also a huge adjustment for parents to let their child marry someone outside their community, caste and religion. Some readily embrace their children's in-laws, but most struggle to accept someone from an entirely different socioreligious systems. They might speak different languages, might not associate readily, and subscribe to different culture, rituals and traditions.

The earlier you realize that marriage is for holiness more than happiness, the better off you are. Marriage creates the best environment in which I can serve God and grow in the character of Christ. When we marry for happiness, we are always evaluating how our mates did not measure up in the relationship or focused on our mates' failures. Contrarily when we marry for holiness, we are more focused on our own failures and how we did not measure up within the marriage. In the first case, it leads to disappointment with my mate and in the later, you recognize God's ideals for you. In the former I am trying to change my mate (that is exactly what your mate is trying to do to you), and results in conflicts. Conversely in the later, I am not trying to change my mate but trying to improve myself and my perspective. Do you see how a divine third person in the marriage improves marriage and both parties involved?

Churches that encourage pro-marriage and pro-family attitudes within their congregation, provide marriage counseling, enrichment and support for newly-married couples. They make the effort to understand family issues and cultural attitudes toward marriage. They should preserve the definition of marriage as a union of one man and one woman. Some of the recent attempts to redefine marriage could create a fundamental crevice, not only in the institution of marriage, but also the church. Healthy marriages make healthy families and healthy families make healthy church. Both faith and family are mutually obligated to serve each other.

Faith Practices: Diligence

Spiritual practices are essential to building intimacy in marriages. Praying together, Bible studies, church worship, family devotions, fasting and other religious rituals bind a couple together with cords that cannot be broken. Making space for God in your life and marriage is vital. Engaging in exercises that help you draw closer to God helps marriages. The closer you are to God, closer you will be to your mate.

The most difficult thing in a marriage is to serve the other person when your own needs aren't being met. That's why marriage is the perfect environment for spiritual development, because it's only when your needs aren't getting met that you begin to work on your overblown sense of self. When the romance and novelty wears off and conflicts become unbearable, the suffering begins in marriage. The suffering we experience in marriage, those unmet needs, and really lonely times, can lead us to the deeper spiritual pursuits. This also happen when we sacrificially serve our mates.

Spiritual practices bring vitality to marriage. Do not push God to the backburner. Intentionally nurture a dynamic personal spirituality and you will be amazed what it can do to your marriage relationship. Set aside time to be alone with God and maintain small group and communal level gathering at regular frequency. By realizing only God can meet our deepest needs, we cultivate more realistic expectations of each other and that we are not solely responsible for each other's happiness! Our individual quiet times also open the door for God to show us things that are pertinent to each of us individually.

Finally, remember that God is the One who is bringing you together with your mate in marriage. He put you two together and he isn't a God who goes halfway. He doesn't give up on something he's started. God is for your marriage. Let God be the glue in your relationship, for he created marriage and knows and will help you build it as well.

If you are still single, look to God for your mate. The One who saw the loneliness of Adam and created Eve and brought her to Adam, will lead you to your life partner. Pursue to draw close to God and discern his heart for your life and future marriage. Live contentedly in your singleness and fulfill God's greater purpose through this stage of life as well. And wait on God, he will renew your strength like the eagles.

Exercise 11: Faith Experiences

1. Do you believe in God? If yes, what do you believe about God? If not, why?

2. What kind of religious upbringing did you have?

3. What faith traditions do your parents/siblings follow now?

4. What are your current religious affiliations [church/fellowship/small groups]? How long have you been involved?

5. What do you on a Sunday or religious holiday? What religious observances do you keep?

6. What role does God play in your life today?

7. What spiritual practices do you engage in and how it benefits you?

8. What has caused spiritual growth or what has hindered growth in you?

9. What are some of the major spiritual milestone in your life?

10. Discuss the people, programs, or institutions that played a major role in your spiritual journey.

Commitment Matters
Making Marriage Last a Lifetime

A successful marriage requires falling in love many times, always with the same person. (Unknown)

So guard the spirit of marriage within you. Don't cheat on your spouse. (Malachi 2:15b, MSG)

Anika's big day had finally arrived. She was getting married to Vikas later that evening. They got engaged nearly a year ago and had carefully planned through every detail of their wedding. All arrangements were going without a glitch, except for the strange uneasiness she felt inside of her. When her mother came into her room to help her with her hairdressing, Anika blurted out, "What if it does not last?"

"What do you mean?" her mother enquired.

"I mean, marriage. What if I am making a wrong decision? What if I am not the one for him and he for me?" Anika sounded genuinely puzzled.

Mother thought Anika was expressing some last minute

wedding jitters. Then thought about her own marriage to Anika's father. Several times they were in near–divorce scenarios and the children had known all about it. But her parents decided to stay together for the sake of kids and their marriage prospects.

As Anika reflected on her parent's troubled marriage and she wondered if the same would happen to her. Anika's mother comforted the daughter, "You don't worry about anything. If it does not work out, you can always come back home here."

Anika burst into sobs saying, "No Mom, I want this to work somehow."

After gathering herself again, she continued, "Mom, thanks for trying to reassure me; but I really don't want to come back here. I want my marriage with Vikas to work. But what if we are not made for each other? I am so afraid that we do not have what it takes to make this last a lifetime. Is it realistic in this day and age? Is it too much to ask for?"

> To have and to hold, from this day forward, for better or for worse, for richer, for poorer, in sickness and in health, to love and cherish; and I promise to be faithful to you, forsaking all others, until death do us part.

Every bride and groom walks down the aisle on the big day, hoping that his/her vows would last lifetime. Every young person longs for a fairy tale ending, but "happily ever after" is more of distant dream for so many couples, who start out well yet do not know how to make it go the distance. Making a marriage go the distance is becoming harder than ever before. Commitment to anything is becoming a rarity. The "use and throw" culture has profoundly invaded our sentimentalities. People always want to keep their options open and do not want to be bound by their past decisions.

Commitment is important because we act differently when we know that our future is tied together. Commitment will help you make peace with your differences, each other's pasts, conflicts that will arise and challenges that are bound to come your way. Commitment is imperative to marital longevity and vitality.

Commitment: What Is It Anyway?

Commitment need not be an old fashioned word. It is imperative to happiness in marriage and will help you stretch your marriage over a lifetime. It is a promise to be there for each other, which generates security and surety and which in turn, helps any marriage flourish beyond your wildest dreams.

Commitment is not just about reciting marriage vows or having a piece of paper that says "marriage license." Lifelong commitment will force us to relate to each other differently. You may avoid a prickly conversation; you will not move on to another love if your current one has a debilitating accident or simply starts to rub you the wrong way. Commitment means you've promised to stay and work it through, not just today, but forever. It means that a couple is in it for life. There is no quitting, or changing

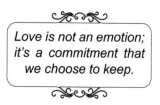

Love is not an emotion; it's a commitment that we choose to keep.

course, no matter what. You are in it, no matter what lies in the future. There is no second guessing or "plan B." We are expected to make it work or die trying, but we are not giving up. There is no revisiting the issue or reconsideration whatsoever. It is a binding and permanent agreement. There is no *force majeure* and failure is not an option.

Commitment is a choice to give up choices. Although this might at first sound limiting, it actually brings greater freedom and depth. No longer does the committed person need to weigh which person or way of life will bring more happiness. Once committed, all of one's energy goes into making this commitment work. No longer are other possibilities a distraction.

Lack of commitment is typical of live-in relationships. Cohabitating couples want all the benefits of relationship, but do not want to make any commitments. The nature of cohabitation presumes the possibility of the relationship not working out and thus commitment is not permanent. If that is what a couple believes at the start of their relationship, that is precisely where they will end up also. If the couple later marries, it can be more of a "sliding into marriage" than a "deciding to marry." The decision to marry becomes less distinct but more of a gradual slide and blurs the clarity of the commitment.

Couples who understand the essence of making a permanent commitment realize that it's much more than just a decision not to divorce. It's a commitment to do the daily work of keeping the commitment alive. It may mean turning off the TV or taking a nightly walk in order to listen to each other's concerns. It might mean not stonewalling your mate or allowing cave time to your mate when he/she returns from work. These simple actions and others are the real stuff of commitment. They are the actions that keep a marriage vibrant, interesting, and exciting so that temptations to make another choice don't erupt. Every day we recommit to each other and the relationship. It is never a onetime pronouncement in a solemn gathering, but daily outworking and following through of that public declaration until the last breath of your life.

Designer's View: Covenant

In the contemporary culture, the word commitment has lost its meaning, but according to the divine Designer, marriage is a sacred covenant. It is the most intimate promise we will ever make to another person, and when a person fails to uphold such a promise everything else seems to have bleak possibility of ever succeeding.

In the biblical times, a very unique ceremony took place when a man and a woman got married. The fathers of the couple would take cows, sheep, birds, goats and would cut the animals in half and put them about ten feet apart, leaving a bloody path. The couple would then walk barefoot through the bloody path saying with their actions, "May I pay with my life if this covenant is broken." When they got married, their attitude was that it is better to be dead than to break the vow of marriage. They were committed to each other for lifetime.

God himself modeled such covenant making when he made an unconditional, unilateral agreement with Abraham. (Read Genesis 15:7-21 for details of this narrative.) God has often depicted his relationship with Israel as a covenant marriage. The prophet Ezekiel called Israel as an adulterous wife whom God longs for "*. . .I spread the corner of my garment over you and covered your nakedness. I gave you my solemn oath and entered into a covenant with you, declares the Sovereign* Lord, *and you became mine*" (16:8). God asked prophet Hosea to marry a prostitute to show the nation of Israel its unfaithfulness and God's steadfast love towards her (Hosea 3:1–3). Through the prophet Malachi, God expressed his displeasure at divorce saying, Lord *is acting as the witness*

"Haven't you read in your Bible that the Creator originally made man and woman for each other, male and female?. . . Because God created this organic union of the two sexes, no one should desecrate his art by cutting them apart."
– Matthew 19:4, 6, MSG.

between you and the wife of your youth, because you have broken faith with her, though she is your partner, the wife of your marriage covenant (Malachi 2:14).

In the creation order, the passage of golden rule of marriage (Genesis 2:24, 25) portrays a picture of permanence in marriage. The Hebrew word for "joined" is *dabaq*, which means "to adhere," "to cling," "to cleave," or "to stick." It means to be joined together in a lasting bond. The New Testament quotes of this verse use the Greek word *kallao*, which literally means "to be glued together." It does not mean being stuck together like post-it notes that you can pull it off and stick again in another place. I understand it as superglue, a deeply intertwining of two lives together that cannot be separated without ripping apart pieces of each other.

Then in the New Testament, Jesus used the imagery of himself as the groom and his church as the bride: *"The kingdom of heaven is like a king who prepared a wedding banquet for his son* (Matthew 22:2). Thus, because Jesus is our husband we have this powerful promise: *"Never will I leave you; never will I forsake you"* (Hebrews 13:5). Jesus still remains an ideal model for any husband, who not only makes a promise not to leave his bride, but was putting his life on the line in order to sanctify his bride.

Without God, such a commitment to one person for life is impossible. God established the order of marriage as a covenant and modeled the covenant for us. Only with God's help can you establish a covenant relationship with your mate. Having the covenant–keeping God at the center of your relationship brings a covenant nature to your relationship. Do not reduce marriage to mere humanistic view where your convenience, pleasure and choice are overriding parameters. Refrain from the temptation to settle for anything less than what marriage was originally designed as and for.

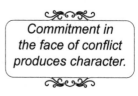

Commitment in the face of conflict produces character.

Character Test

Commitment flows out of character. The word commitment can be defined as "devotion or dedication to a cause, person or relationship." In the Scriptures, word "committed" refers to surrendering or yielding. It implies that one literally gives over to another and is "locked away." A man–woman relationship before the wedding should be marked with growing commitment between the couple, resulting in the marriage vow or ceremonial bonding whatever tradition you might have at your wedding. Pre-marital sex and other momentary pleasures threaten lifelong marital happiness and are indicative of a lack of character. By character, we mean genuine love, the ability to forgive each other's offenses, emotional and sexual purity, being patient or having ability to endure each other's weakness, being kind and generous towards each other, and integrity.

Character provides dependability and deep trust. If boundaries were not respected and upheld before marriage, it is less likely to be so after the wedding. Even for the most committed husband or wife, there comes times when they see someone else across a crowded room that is prettier or more handsome or wittier or easier to get along with than the one he/she has married. And for a brief ugly moment they wonder, "what if I had married him or her?' Temptation and other alternatives are not going to disappear because you got married.

You might be thinking that if relationship works and everything works as you had dreamed then you will commit. But that is upside down logic. The secret to a lasting marriage is that you commit to the marriage first and then you will see how everything works out. There is no trial run or test-driving in marriage, though some try cohabitation to test their compatibility, which has repeatedly proven to be a serious impediment to a happy marriage. Only if it begins with commitment, will we be able to really reap its dividends and make it last.

You may be thinking, "How can anyone commit to anything like that?" Should not one have the freedom to choose based on future realities? How can anyone decide for rest of their lives at a given point? What happens when marriage isn't working anymore? Isn't it foolish to blindly commit without knowing the details? Every marital commitment should be characterized by an unconditional promise for the benefit of the recipient. It begins with giving and provides room for confrontation and forgiveness. At the core of commitment between married couples is steadfast love and servanthood. Each spouse is committed to the well–being of the others. It brings other-centeredness and defeats our selfishness. Both refuse to focus on the negative aspects of each other and gives verbal affirmations of their positive traits. The attitude with which you enter marriage and how you see your mate will ascertain marital quality. Develop a heart of commitment and express that repeatedly to your mate. Who would not like a relationship like that?

Fear of Commitment: Is It Real?

Before I (Sam) made a mental and verbal commitment to Mary, I struggled with the whole idea of commitment for a while. I have always believed marriage should be for a lifetime. As I got married late and was an eligible bachelor for a prolonged period of time, several marriage proposals used to come to me and my parents. I would brush them aside saying "I am not ready." When parents began to put pressure, I evaded them by getting busier at work.

Both men and women live longer, happier, healthier and wealthier lives when they are married. Unmarried co-habitation doesn't cut it. Cohabitation does not bring the benefits—in physical health, wealth, and emotional wellbeing—that marriage does. And, married people have both more and better sex than do their unmarried counterparts.
– Linda Waite (The Case for Marriage)

During my corporate career days, I was disillusioned by the marriages that I saw among my friends, colleagues, and clients. Sure, I had a rather big job and traveled extensively and I did not have any time to get married or settle down. But much deeper issue was that of commitment. I wondered how anyone could absolutely be sure to make a decision for rest of your life. Moreover, I had several divorced colleagues and bosses, and I was fearful that the same would happen to me. I reasoned, "If this is the lifestyle they had and knowing how busy they were. . .and if I go down that path,

I am sure to end where they have ended up." Seeing many broken or troubled marriages can disenchant your idea of marriage itself.

Though both genders struggle in this area, men tend to struggle more. For many guys, the very thought of making a commitment to one woman for the rest of their lives is enough to send them sprinting to the hills. The dreaded "C–word" implies compromise, loss of independence, the sacrifice of sexual variety, and the looming specter of lifelong bondage.

Men love their freedom and are extremely independent by nature. Making a commitment to a woman in marriage, would mean getting the permission of your wife for everything you want to do when you want to do it. Men feel they cannot make their own decisions and run their lives by their own rules. For men, marriage also means cutting themselves off from any other sexual pursuits. Men do not want to take responsibility for a wife and family. If they can have to have sex without marriage, they see no reason to be bound by the commitment that marriage requires. They fear sexual boredom and a total lack of desire. No wonder they dread the idea of making a commitment to a person for life.

For women, the fear of commitment generally entails fear of exposure and marital happiness. It could come in the form of panic attacks or frightening nightmares. To some extent we all struggle through making a lifelong commitment to our mates. We have counseled many young men and women who have struggled with marital commitment. The "commitment phobia" is rooted in fear, fear of lost options or fear of making poor decisions. It sees opening the possibility of being caged or trapped forever with no means of escape. Commitment phobia is a real disabling fear. Some don't trust their judgment and vacillate between certainty and doubt or fear making the next step because of an unresolved issue from past failures. Some others move toward commitment too quickly and still others worry that something bad may happen. Some form of fear haunts everyone as they approach marriage.

Getting close to another person in total transparency is a scary thing. It means opening yourself up and making yourself vulnerable. It means making the space for the other person to open up to you, and making an effort to understand him or her. You must conquer your fear of commitment. You should try to sift through the real fears from those that were unimportant or anxiety–driven. You should know who you are and what you wanted in your mate, then commitment would be relatively easier.

Contrary to the popular view, in the context of total commitment you and your mate are free to develop greater levels of intimacy and connection. The undying devotion to each other and to God is a trait of a strong marriage. In fact, commitment of a couple to each other is derivative of one's commitment to the Lord. The stronger we grow in our commitment with Jesus Christ, the stronger the marriage relationship will be.

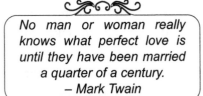

No man or woman really knows what perfect love is until they have been married a quarter of a century.
– Mark Twain

Greener Grass Syndrome

The contemporary culture values choices and keeping all options open. People say not to get tied down to anything and not to give up anything. We tend to bring the same attitude to our marriages as well. But, marital commitment involves making the choice to give up other choices and sticking with the choice you have made by protecting it for the rest of your life.

Making the commitment is not confined to the wedding day promise you make to your mate; is to live that promise everyday thereafter. We all tend to compare our mates with others and find them more attractive. It is akin to looking over the fence and thinking that grass is greener on the other side of the fence. If you are constantly working on your marriage, you are less likely to be drawn to explore other alternatives.

Unless we build hedges of protection around our marriage, every couple is vulnerable to breaking that sacred vow. We should be aware of the dangers of this syndrome in order to protect our marriages. You should avoid hanging around the fence and comparing the grass with your neighbors' lawn. Build higher hedges so you will not be tempted to look in that direction constantly. Take care of your own lawn (marriage) so that you will not be looking elsewhere. Pull out weeds, water and fertilize your garden to have a lush green grass in your own yard. Remember, hedges are living things unlike wooden or barbed wire fences. If you trim and water it, the hedges will grow tall and strong to protect your relationship.

Commitment to marriage encompasses a commitment to marital exclusivity, indissolubility, fruitfulness, and the like. Personal dedication and normative commitment also entail a set of virtues that make the goods of marriage possible—such as fidelity, loyalty, generosity, and fortitude. Regardless of whether one marries in a secular or religious ceremony most couples still believe that they are making a permanent commitment.

Marriage research has shown that many marriages could be revived if the commitment is strong. In one of the study a large sample of unhappily married couples found that after five years, four fifths of the formerly unhappy couples reported that they were very happy or quite happy. Sometimes it is simply the commitment to each other that carries a couple through the harder times, along with generous doses of time, counseling, effort, luck, and faith.

Love is a decision. To follow through with a decision we require a commitment. The feeling of love is not sufficient for a fulfilling marriage. A husband and wife need to decide to love, even when they don't feel like it or the other is unlovable. That calls for commitment. Acting on this decision by doing loving things for your spouse, speaking kindly and respectfully, and deciding over and over to pay attention to the relationship makes love rekindle.

The Christian custom of placing a wedding ring on the third

finger began with the Greeks. The early Greeks believed that a certain vein, the "vein of love," ran from the third finger directly to the heart. Why they thought that way no one knows, but when you put those rings on each other's ring finger part of you are symbolically saying that you wanted to be twined right into their hearts and be committed to each other.

Now, when the early Christians exchanged rings, they worked their way across the hand beginning with the index finger and ending with the ring finger. The groom first placed the ring on the tip of the bride's index finger, praying "in the name of the Father," moved it to her middle finger saying, "in the name of the Son," and finally, with the words "and of the Holy Spirit, Amen," he slipped the ring on the to the third finger. In the giving of the ring, the early Christian was saying his marriage would begin with his commitment to God.

We began this chapter with Anika's dilemma and let's finish with rest of the story. Across town, her fiancé Vikas also woke up on that special day with great anticipation, the day for which they both were waiting. Vikas came from a strong Christian family and was himself a committed Christian, very active in the local church and ministries. Vikas had met Anika at a local Christian music concert and began to interact on and off.

Vikas had prayed about his relationship with Anika and felt that this was of the Lord. He sought advice from his parents, pastor and close believing friends. Over the last year or so, their relationship had grown closer and several circumstantial evidences seem to point in one direction—marriage. The feeling and conviction was mutual. A year ago, he expressed his desire to marry her and she agreed enthusiastically. They were officially engaged a month later and everyone who had known them, including his parents and relatives were extremely happy and sensed the Lord's hand on this relationship.

I (Sam) had known both of them individually and they expressed their desire to get married to each other. They came to us for pre-marital training and we worked through several resources together. In spite of several challenges that lay before them, they did a reasonably good job in preparing for the marriage along with their wedding planning. I was honored when they asked me if I could briefly speak at their wedding, to which I agreed.

On the wedding day, as the officiating priest and myself reached Vikas' home to pray, before leaving for the church as was the custom in that community, Vikas invited us to come to his room along with his father and younger brother. He closed the door and said, "I want to share something with you all. Today I am going to make a commitment to Anika before God and you all. I believe it is a sacred thing and I am bound by it for rest of my life. With God's help, I want to be all that I am and can be in this marriage. No matter what lay ahead, I am committed to Anika as long as I am alive. From this day on, I remove 'divorce' from my vocabulary. I would request you all to hold me accountable to this commitment."

My eyes welled up, as I saw the deep sincerity and love of this young man. All five of us took turns to hug him and we knelt down to pray for Vikas and Anika. The power of that moment is etched in my mind. No matter what Anika's fears were and all the uncertainties of the future, I knew this couple will go the distance.

Commitment makes all the difference and its security helps marriage not only go the distance, but help it to flourish to the fullest potential. Are you ready for such a commitment?

Exercise 12: Life Commitment

1. What kind of strong commitment have you seen that made an impression on you?

2. What kind of failed commitment have you seen?

3. How secure do you feel in God's commitment to you?

4. Describe commitment of your parent's marriage? Also marriage of siblings and friends?

5. What fears do you have about making a total commitment to your mate?

6. What are some ways that you can express commitment to your mate?

7. What are some ways that your mate has expressed commitment to you?

8. How anxious are you about the security of the commitment with your fiancé(e)?

9. How did/will you know that you were/are ready to make a lasting commitment to your mate?

10. What would you do to follow through or renew your commitment to your mate? How often?

Conclusion
Wrapping Up

Grow old along with me. The best is yet to be—the last of life for which the first was made. (Robert Browning)

He who finds a wife finds what is good. (Proverbs 18:22)

It is sad to note that years of education does not prepare most young people for one of the most important, life changing and momentous events in their lives, marriage. Most couples walking down the aisle or tying the sacred thread or signing papers in court are clueless about real marriage entails. For a girl, it means giving up her childhood home and moving into another. To a boy, it means taking on the responsibility of caring for and providing for another person. Marriage involves adapting to new personalities, cultures, even cuisines! And this incredible life-event comes without a course, a qualification or an instruction manual!

That's why we wrote this book. We have been blessed with a great marriage, and we were eternally grateful to God for this adventure.

We had the benefit of countless resources on marriage and wisdom of several godly couples who have great marriages. From early in our marriage, we have been helping others to get a great start in their marriage, and in this book, we try to capture some of those lessons for you.

To be happily married takes more than finding the person and hoping for some good luck. Good marriages could be the most fulfilling aspect of life on earth, and you need a great deal of time and effort in developing it. When we understand God's design of marriage and work within its framework, we will experience great joy and meaning in our marriage.

Whether you are a single adult seriously thinking about a relationship or an engaged couple counting down your days to the big day, we believe marital preparation helps immensely in building a lasting and fulfilling marriage. If you are not in any relationship yet, we hope this has helped you gain a deeper understanding of marriage and what you could do at your end, before getting into a committed relationship. Being proactive, and learning about marriage and having a realistic view of marriage will help you get a great start.

We hope what we shared here has helped you. Please take time to work through the exercises and reflect on the questions. After every exercise discuss your thoughts and answers with your mate. Do not rush through it. Make copious amount of journal entries and share them with your mate. This is crucial to developing intimacy with your mate. Hold yourself accountable to an older couple you both know and respect. Take time to discuss some of the marriage concepts with parents, married friends, role models, pastors and other authority figures in your community. We hope and pray that you will go on to build a Christ-centered, God-honoring and mutually fulfilling marriage.

Godspeed!

Recommended Resources

Marriage Preparation

1. Dennis Rainey, (Editor). *Preparing for Marriage.* Gospel Light, Ventura, CA, 1997.
2. Les & Leslie Parrot. *Saving Your Marriage before It Starts.* Zondervan, Grand Rapids, MI, 1995.
3. H. Norman Wright. *So, You Are Getting Married.* Regal Books, Ventura, CA, 1985.
4. David Olson & Amy Olson. *Empowering Couples.* Life Innovations, Minneapolis, MN, 2000.
5. Bill & Lynne Hybels. *Fit to Be Tied.* Zondervan, Grand Rapids, MI, 1991.
6. Robert & Alice Fryling. *A Handbook for Engaged Couples.* IVP, Downers Grove, IL, 1996.
7. Niel Clark Warren. *Finding the Love of Your Life.* Focus on the Family, Colorado Springs, CO, 1992.
8. Dale & Susan Mathis. *Countdown for Couples.* Tyndale, Carol Streams, IL, 2008.

Christian Marriage

1. Walter Trobish. *I Married You.* Quiet Waters Publications, Bolivar, MO, 1971.
2. Gary Thomas. *Sacred Marriage.* Zondervan Publishing, Grand Rapids, MI, 2002.
3. Walter Wangerin. *As for Me and My House.* Nelson, Nashville, TN, 1990.
4. Jack & Judith Balswick. *A Model for Marriage.* IVP, Downer's Grove, IL, 2006.
5. Dan Allender & Tremper Longman III. *The Intimate Marriage.* IVP, Downers Grove, IL, 2005.
6. James Dobson. *Love for a Lifetime.* Random House, Colorado Springs, CO, 2003.

7. Ravi Zacharias. *I Isaac, Take Thee Rebekah.* Thomas Nelson, Nashville, TN, 2004.
8. Steve Stephens. *Blueprints for a Solid Marriage.* Tyndale, Carol Streams, IL, 2006.

Relationships

1. Henry Cloud & John Townsend. *Boundaries.* Zondervan, Grand Rapids, MI, 1992.
2. Daniel Goleman. *Emotional Intelligence.* Bantam Books, New York, NY, 1997.
3. John Gottman. *Why Marriages Succeed or Fail.* Simon Schuster, New York, NY, 1994.
4. Les & Leslie Parrot. *Becoming Soul Mates.* Zondervan, Grand Rapids, MI, 1995.
5. Willard Harley. *His Needs, Her Needs.* Revell, Nashville, TN, 2004.
6. Dennis Rainey. *Building Your Mate's Self-Esteem.* Thomas Nelson, TN, 1996.
7. Philip Swihart & Wilford Wooten, (Editors). *The Complete Guide to the First Five Years of Marriage.* Tyndale, Carol Stream, IL, 2006.
8. Al Janssen. *Marriage Masterpiece.* Tyndale, Carol Stream, IL, 2008.

Communication & Finances

1. Norman Wright. *Communications: Key to Your Marriage.* Regal, Ventura, CA, 2000.
2. Les & Leslie Parrott. *Love Talk.* Zondervan, Grand Rapids, MI, 2005.
3. Larry Burkett. *Money before Marriage.* Moody Publishers, Chicago, IL, 1996.
4. Ron Blue. *Taming the Money Monster.* Living Books, 2000
5. Cary Chapman. *Five Love Languages.* Northfield Publishing, Chicago, IL, 1992.

6. Emerson Eggerichs. *Love and Respect.* Integrity, Brentwood, TN, 2004.

7. Ed Wheat, M.D. and Gaye Wheat, *Intended for Pleasure: Sex Technique and Sexual Fulfillment in Christian Marriage,* Revell, Grand Rapids, MI, 1997.

8. Clifford & Joyce Penner. *The Gift of Sex.* Thomas Nelson, TN, 2003.

Devotionals

1. Dennis & Barbara Rainey. *FamilyLife Marriage Bible.* Thomas Nelson, Nashville, TN, 2007.

2. Dennis & Barbara Rainey. *Moments Together for Couples.* Regal, Colorado Springs, CO, 1994.

3. James Dobson. *Night Light.* Tyndale, Carol Streams, IL, 2003.

4. Stormie Omartian. *Power of a Praying Wife.* Harvest House, Eugene, OR, 1997.

5. Stormie Omartian, *Power of a Praying Husband.* Harvest House, Eugene, OR, 2001.

Web

1. PREP (Preparation and Relationship Enhancement) program—www.prepinc.com

2. Couple Communication—www.couplecommunication.com

3. PAIRS (Practical Application of Intimate Relationship Skills)—www.pairs.com

4. PREPARE (Premarital Education by Life Innovation)—www.prepare-enrich.com

5. Real Relationships— www.realrelationships.com

6. Marriage Preparation Course—www.themarriagecourse.org

7. Focus on the Family—www.family.org

8. Familylife Ministries—www.familylife.com

9. Parivar International—www.ParivarInternational.org

10. Urban India Ministries—www.UrbanIndia.org

INTERNATIONAL

Building Strong Families One Home At A Time

PARIVAR International is a US-based charitable family organization committed to building strong families in the Asian Indian community worldwide. "Parivar" means family in many of the Indian languages. PARIVAR is a Christian ministry committed to serve all in the Asian Indian community regardless of caste, creed, color, nationality or religion.

We offer a wide range of educational and enrichment events like premarital training, marriage seminars and family retreats. We also offer counseling to hurting individuals and families. We are continually developing resources to help families thrive.

For more on premarital resources and programs, please visit www.theweddingbells.org

Family Helpline (in US):
1-877-PHELP-11(1-877-743-5711)
info@ParivarInternational.org

Parivar International
P.O. Box 5301
Vernon Hills, IL – 60061.
Phone:(847)-362-1804

www.ParivarInternational.org